JASPER JOHNS
THE SCULPTURES

JASPER JOHNS
THE SCULPTURES

AN EXHIBITION ORGANISED BY
THE CENTRE FOR THE STUDY OF SCULPTURE AT
THE HENRY MOORE INSTITUTE IN LEEDS

Jasper Johns : The Sculptures

Published in Great Britain
to accompany an exhibition at

The Menil Collection, Houston
16 February – 31 March 1996

and at

Leeds City Art Gallery
18 April – 29 June 1996

Prepared and published by
The Centre for the Study of Sculpture
Henry Moore Institute
74 The Headrow
Leeds LS1 3AA

© The Henry Moore Institute and the author

Edited by Penelope Curtis

Designed by Groundwork, Skipton

Printed and bound in Great Britain

ISBN 1 900081 50 4

The works of Jasper Johns are copyright
© Jasper Johns/DACS, London/VAGA, New York 1996

Photographic credits:
Rudolph Burckhardt pp. 10, 13, 46, 61, 65, 68, 71, 73, 77,
78, 80, 81, 83, 85, 89, 91, 92, 95, 97, 98, 100, 101
Bevan Davies pp. 56, 96
© 1996 The Museum of Modern Art, New York p. 13
Eric Pollitzer p. 84
Pollitzer, Strong & Meyer pp. 54, 58
Lee Stalsworth p. 8
Glenn Steigelman Inc pp. 86, 89
Jim Strong p. 64
Universal Limited Art Editions Inc. p. 39
Dorothy Zeidman pp. 45, 52, 72, 74, 75, 76, 79,
82, 87, 88, 90, 93, 94

CONTENTS

PREFACE

Many people have remarked to us that it seems surprising that there has not already been an exhibition devoted to the sculptures of Jasper Johns. As we are a Centre for the Study of Sculpture, it is not, however, surprising, that we should now be addressing that situation. Jasper Johns is, of course, a painter first and foremost, but his sculptural output is not negligible and indeed informs our understanding of his 2-dimensional works; just as those feed into his sculpture. Thus the present exhibition can be seen to be part of a developing series here in which we focus on a marginal but nonetheless significant component within an artist's oeuvre.

It was Fred Orton, at the University of Leeds, who proposed this exhibition. He has made the selection with Jasper Johns, and many of the sculptures come from the studio itself. This means not only that several have never previously been exhibited, but that they are in fact the working models for the subsequent casts. We are immensely grateful to Mr Johns for entrusting us with this kind of very private material.

Fred Orton has embraced this project with infectious enthusiasm. He has previously written on Johns' painting, but not on his sculpture, and indeed this text is the first that he has written about any kind of sculpture. It has been fun to have been a part of that particular journey, and I think we, as readers, benefit from the resulting freshness of the text, which takes us through Orton's looking, very carefully, step by step.

Fred Orton makes it clear to us how sculpture had different meanings for Johns at different times. Johns' moments of making sculpture coincide with moments in art-history, with moments in his own painting, as well as with moments of more personal significance. Orton's text takes us from the concentrated group of sculptures, from around 1960, through the occasional, but significant, occurrence of sculpture in the years thereafter.

We were fortunate that Sarah Taggart, at Jasper Johns' Studio, took up this project with such interest. We owe a great deal to her care and attention to detail. We owe a different, but no less important, debt to the lenders who have been generous enough to help us realise the aim of the exhibition. We must particularly acknowledge the Philadelphia Museum of Art, where a group of sculptures has been specially removed from semi-permanent display.

This project was originally conceived for Leeds alone, but when, by a combination of circumstances, it was mooted that it also be shown at The Menil Collection in Houston, we realised that we should take up the opportunity to present the show on both sides of the Atlantic. For the Henry Moore Institute in England it is a welcome chance to disseminate our activities more widely, and we acknowledge the part played in this by Paul Winkler, Director of The Menil Collection.

When one visits the Philadelphia Museum one is inevitably struck by the Duchamp Gallery. On my visit there I was particularly struck by Duchamp's casts from 1950* onwards. They felt close to me as Johns' sculptures felt close. I asked Jasper Johns to define this proximity, and he did so in terms of scale. Both Duchamp's and Johns' sculptures are, indeed, exactly life size, and beyond their essential quiddity, they are also of a scale for handling. But Duchamp's pieces are close to us because they fit us; they seal, stop or plug. Johns' pieces on the other hand are not of us, they are in front of us, and it is in this apartness that their intrigue lies. I hope that this exhibition, and this catalogue, will play their part in bringing these sculptures closer to us, while reaffirming their status as objects for looking.

Penelope Curtis

Curator, Centre for the Study of Sculpture

---

* *Feuille de vigne femelle* 1950, *Objet Dard* 1951, *Bouche-Evier* 1964 (and also *Coin de chasteté* 1954), casts which, interestingly enough, were also made from and for his friends.

Fig. 1
Untitled, 1954, painted wood, plaster cast and collage
on canvas with glass, 26$^{1}/_{4}$" × 8$^{3}/_{4}$". Hirshhorn Museum
and Sculpture Garden, Smithsonian Institution, Regents
Collections Acquisition Programme, with matching
funds from the Thomas M. Evans, Jerome L. Greene,
Joseph H. Hirshhorn, and Sydney and Frances Lewis
Purchase Fund, 1987.

JASPER JOHNS: THE SCULPTURES

FRED ORTON [1]

One of the crucial problems in art is the business of 'meaning it'. If you are a painter, meaning the paintings you make; if you are an observer, meaning what you see. It is very difficult for us to mean what we say or do. We would like to, but society makes this very hard for us to succeed in doing.

Jasper Johns to Joseph E. Young, 1969[2]

Plaster   *Conversing in a room that had both painting and sculpture in it and knowing as he does that there is a difference between them, he suddenly laughed for he heard what he had just said (I am not a sculptor). I felt suddenly lost, and then speaking to me as though I were a jury he said: But I* am *a sculptor, am I not?*

John Cage, 'Jasper Johns: Stories and Ideas', 1964[3]

In 1954, Jasper Johns, a year or so out of the army, living in New York at East Eighth Street and Avenue C and about to make the decision that he was an artist – and destroy whatever work was in his possession that he had produced up to that time – made a plaster life mask of his friend Rachel Rosenthal.[4] Then, or perhaps a short while afterwards, he put the cast in the lower of two compartments in a crude wooden box painted white. In the upper compartment there is a collaged panel that was positioned slightly forward of the box's backboard and completely fills – fits tightly into – its rear surface area. This collage presents a variegated and veiled collection of textual and pictorial matter. The upper compartment is covered with a sheet of glass held in place with six small nails. This object is usually referred to as *Untitled Construction* (fig. 1), a title, maybe not given to it by Johns, that gives nothing away concerning its meanings or effects. It is not known whether the cast was made for the box or whether the box was made for the cast or whether they came together contingently. Johns produced at least one more box-like construction in 1954: a cross-shaped object made, like *Untitled Construction*, of a thick wooden frame with a collage base, all painted white, and covered with glass. *Star* (The Menil Collection, Houston), made in 1955, is a close relative.[5] And more plaster casts might also have been made.

Fig. 2
Target with Plaster Casts, 1955,
encaustic and collage on canvas with objects,
51" × 44" × 3¹/₂".
The David Geffen Collection, Los Angeles.

Johns carried on making plaster casts when, towards the end of 1954 or at the start of 1955, he moved into a studio on Pearl Street. At least seven of them, casts of body parts taken from several male and female friends and acquaintances, 'happened to be around in the studio' in the summer of 1955 and got taken into the row of boxes with hinged lids that he attached to the top of the blue and yellow 'target' in the red field that together make up the large construction known as *Target with Plaster Casts* (fig. 2).[6] The casts are not easy to make out because each one is painted the same colour as the box it has come to occupy: a purple foot; white nose and lips; a red hand with the little finger missing; a pink breast; an orange ear; a green penis and scrotum; and a yellow heel. There is also a black bone. One box is empty but for some collage-plastering on its sides. Also in 1955, possibly immediately after he had made *Target with Plaster Casts*, Johns made another 'target' construction, this time using four plaster life masks he had taken − not from Rosenthal − from another friend, Fance Stevenson: *Target with Four Faces* (The Museum of Modern Art, New York).[7] Again the casts were fitted into boxes attached to the top of the 'target'. Each cast is unique. With each successive casting Stevenson relaxed. Johns arranged the casts out of sequence so as not to create a narrative of relaxation or of 'a mouth about to speak'.[8] Each cast has been cut off below the lower lip and above the bridge of the nose seemingly to fit into its box. These are four faces without eyes. A similar but not precisely the same kind of reduction can be seen to have happened to the life mask incorporated in *Target with Plaster Casts*. Unlike that larger 'target' construction, however, here all the casts and the boxes are painted the same colour, a tanfastick orange, and one long lid serves to open and close all the boxes. A subject is being authorised by these works: an artist who is projecting a desire to do something in a characteristic way, who is concerned with the production of something 'other'.

Untitled Construction, *Target with Plaster Casts* and *Target with Four Faces* were produced around the moment that Johns decided to be an artist. The production of a beginning is theoretically and practically tied up with all kinds of complex relations that have to do with conscious and unconscious determinations, with interests and competences, with a subject or subjects (or lack of them), with training (or the lack of it), and so on. At the beginning of this essay I want to draw attention to Johns' interest in making plaster casts, a method and material associated with the practice of sculpture. We might regard this activity as of peripheral interest to him, especially if the casts were made for no other purpose than to make them and keep them 'around in the studio'. It may be significant that, when they were used, they came to occupy places below or above, at the edge of, largish pictorial surfaces, attached to them as a kind of 'editorial sculptural comment'.[9] Casting in plaster, the way Johns did it, is also a rudimentary process. Making a life mask or casting a penis against the scrotum involves none of the complexity of casting in the round and requires not so much skill as technique. Johns had the knack. Nevertheless his interest was there, and the process of taking body casts from himself and friends surely implies that it was a personal, intimate and intense one. It also went beyond the application of technique. A life mask is 'inevitably a frontally conceived "fossil"': a kind of flat impression; an inanimate, almost unmediated equivalent of the thing it comes from and remains in place of.[10] Johns thought of the casts as 'literal representations of things that didn't involve an interpretation'[11], but he always amended and extended their literalism: he broke, cut and snipped them to shape and size, and fitted them to various contexts; he covered and coloured them with paint which not only acted as a preservative but also changed their surface texture. You can't do very much with plaster casts; they are dry and delicate, desiccated and fragile, and that is, in part, why Johns turned them into something else. Good technique gave way to artifice and factitiousness. Their seeming literalism, understood like metaphor as the initial equivocating insight into a whole system of doubly articulated correspondences and proportions, provided the basis for a rhetoric of tropes: relations of parts and wholes running through the work; synecdoches and metonyms; allegory.[12]

At the moment he decided that he was an artist, Johns' practice evidences a predilection for plaster casting. He would sustain this interest in casting but plaster would give way to other materials including bronze and silver, wax and rubber. However, despite this interest in sculptural technique and in using it to make objects like *Untitled Construction* and *Target with Plaster Casts*, the work that is generally taken as Johns' beginning as an artist, and the work that he himself took as his beginning, was not *Untitled Construction* or *Target with Plaster Casts* but the work that came between them in the winter of 1954–1955, *Flag*.

Flag

The words 'flag, standard, colors or ensign', as used herein, shall include any flag, standard, colors, ensign, or any picture or representation of either, or of any part or parts of either, made of any substance or represented on any substance, of any size evidently purporting to be either of said flag, standard, colors, or ensign of the United States of America or a picture or a representation of either, upon which shall be shown the colors, the stars and the stripes, in any number of either thereof, or of any part or parts of either, by which the average person seeing the same without deliberation may believe the same to represent the flag, colors, standard, or ensign of the United States of America.

United States Statutes at Large, 1947[13]

Is it a flag, or is it a painting?

Alan R. Solomon, 'Jasper Johns', 1964[14]

Say, the painting of a flag is always about a flag, but it is no more about a flag than it is about a brush-stroke or about a colour or about the physicality of paint, I think.

Jasper Johns to David Sylvester, 1965[15]

Johns began making *Flag* (fig. 3) with what would have been regarded as respectable, even conventional, avant-garde materials: enamel paints on a bed sheet. But he could not make the paint do what he wanted it to do. When he put the paint on the canvas and then added another brushstroke, the second brushstroke smeared the first, unless he waited until the paint was dry. And the paint took too long to dry. Either he had read about encaustic painting or someone suggested that he use hot wax as a medium because it dried very quickly: as soon as one stroke cooled, he could put on another one and it would not alter what had previously been done.[16] Johns adapted what he knew of encaustic to the collage technique that he had developed in 1954 and used for the panel in *Untitled Construction*.

The process that Johns invented – 'invented' because he uses wax in a way distinct from the way it is used in encaustic painting – involved dipping pieces of newsprint scrap into hot pigmented wax – red, white and blue – and fixing them to the fabric and each other before the wax cooled and solidified. In some places extra coloured wax was brushed on and in other places oil paint was applied, conventionally, with a brush. Each application of wax, with or without newsprint scrap, each dab of paint, is distinct in accent, text and texture from those adjacent to it or under or over it. Johns' use of dabbed paint and separate applications of wax and newsprint enabled him to give the fabric a new uniform surface of something that was neither of painting nor collage but both painting and collage.

Making a painting of a flag is not the same as making one with paint. The former involves the artist in the practice of representing a flag – a flag is the subject-matter that must, according to the theory of modern art with regard to painting that

Fig. 3
Flag, 1954–5, encaustic, oil and collage on fabric mounted on plywood, 42¹/₄" × 60⁵/₈".
The Museum of Modern Art, New York. Gift of Philip Johnson in honour of Alfred H. Barr, Jr.

was dominant in the 1950s, give way to surface matter. The latter means dispensing with the insistence on surface over subject-matter the better to make the object itself in and with paint. From the moment Johns hit on the idea of having the Stars and Stripes provide the precise structure for the way he possessed and used the surface, the idea of making a painting of a flag was compromised. What Johns was doing was more like making a Stars and Stripes than making a painting of one. A major problem must have been how to ensure that what he painted did not fuse with the Stars and Stripes to such an extent that he made the flag of the United States of America. With the change from enamel paints to coloured wax and newsprint scrap he hit on an effective way of preventing that from happening. What prevents *Flag* from becoming the flag of the United States of America is, more than anything else, its fascinating surface.

Leo Steinberg wrote, at the end of 1961, that in Johns' work object and emblem, content and form, subject and surface, subject and picture become so much one and the same – they are held in a kind of 'perpetual oscillation' – that the distinction hardly holds.[17] Alan R. Solomon, in his catalogue essay for the Johns retrospective at the Jewish Museum, New York, in 1964, wrote that the work might be seen as posing 'unanswerable questions' like 'Is it a flag, or is it a painting?'.[18] *Flag* offers us a choice, an 'either' and an 'or'. A year later, when asked which it was, Johns would say that it was 'just a way of beginning… the painting of a flag is always about a flag, but it is no more about a flag than it is about a brush-stroke or about a colour or about the physicality of paint, I think.'[19] The peculiar character of *Flag*, where the Stars and Stripes and the art object are so thoroughly congruent, is such that wherever one looks there is both flag and painting (or something that is neither painting nor collage but simultaneously both painting and collage). Both are in place, and each works to interrupt the effect of the other to an extent that *Flag* seems neither the one nor the other and both. This causes problems for the spectator, and especially for the art critic and art historian who is concerned to fix or attest to its meaning and value. For theoreticians of *Flag* the problem was, and is, how to tell it like it *is* when its *is-ness* is so unstable and uncertain. *Flag* has something of the qualities and effects of an 'undecidable'. It is always neither flag nor painting (or something that is neither painting nor collage but both painting and collage) but both flag and painting (or something that is neither painting nor collage but both painting and collage).[20]

With the first two objects made when he had decided he was an artist, *Flag* and *Target with Plaster Casts*, Johns established two distinct alternatives, continuities or absolutes, from which to project a practice. There has been a tendency to see these two objects as similar in terms of form and facture. They are 'things the mind already knows', the Stars and Stripes and a 'target'.[21] In each case a preestablished arrangement limits and prescribes the use of the surface. And in each case a surface has been applied with the same technique. However, the use of boxed plaster cast body parts makes the effect of *Target with Plaster Casts* different from that of *Flag*. One of the first critics to comment on both works referred to the former as 'a peep-show'.[22] Some of its meaning and value was almost hidden and set apart from the beholder. It provided an occasion for looking furtively or prying; what was to be had from it visually was to be taken away by stealth or secretly or as if by spying. It imposed 'a moral decision on the observer' who, presumably, could either close the lids over the cast body parts or stop looking.[23] Another of the first commentators on Johns' art found that with the lids closed the 'concentration' was on 'the presence and beauty of the target' and that with the lids open there was a 'mystery'.[24] What is the relation between the casts and the target? Disconcerting though this may be, the beholder has some sense of security about what he or she is looking at when he or she looks at *Target with Plaster Casts*. He or she is looking at boxed body parts and a 'target'. Also, he or she is more or less in control of the looking. But something troubles him or her about what is being looked at, and perhaps also about the way he or she is looking at it. This can be made less troubling by closing the lids over the plaster casts. Things get better when the focus is on a whole and not on the whole with the parts. There is, then, a missing unity. In the object and perhaps also in the looking. The body parts and their relation to the 'target' will not add up. They do not represent a whole. Nor is there any satisfactory whole that can be seen as represented in and by the sum of the body parts.[25] It is unwholesome. Unhealthy. Trying to theorise *Target with Plaster Casts*, the critic moves away from seeing and telling the object to speculating about Johns. *Target with Plaster Casts* 'presents another aspect of Johns'.[26] It is a work that, almost inescapably, evokes thoughts about the artist and provokes the psychologising mind to psychology. Steinberg, for example, thought that Johns 'was tracking a dangerous possibility to its limits' and 'miscalculated. Not that he failed to make a picture that works; but the attitude of detachment required to make it work on his stated terms is too special, too rare, and too pitilessly matter-of-fact to acquit the work of morbidity. When affective human elements are conspicuously used, and yet not used as subjects, their subjugation becomes a subject that's got out of control'.[27] What is of interest here is that the disposition hinted at, represented or effected by *Target with Plaster Casts*, was more or less excluded from the progress of Johns' art thereafter.

Flag affects the beholder in a different way. In life the flag of the United States of America interpellates a patriotic public looking that is codified, but in Johns' art it also interpellates an artistic looking that is uncoded and seemingly private. *Flag* interpellates two ways of beholding. Unlike *Target with Plaster Casts*, it does not simply surrender to being looked at or not looked at. Nor does it permit the easy reading-in of psychobiographies. It entangles the beholder in a play of hermeneutic intrigue. In order to see *Flag* it seems necessary to make a decision about what you are looking at – content or form, subject or surface, subject or picture, flag or painting, life or art – even as you are kept off balance and prevented from deciding upon what you are looking at. It is this hermeneutic intrigue that Johns picks up on and tries to develop at his beginning as an artist. And when, three or four years later, he began to produce the objects that he would make as a 'sculptor' rather than as a 'painter', it was *Flag* that set the problem of what to make and how to make it. I wonder what President John F. Kennedy thought he was being given on Flag Day, June 14, 1963, when Leo Castelli presented him with Johns' bronze **Flag** of 1960.[28] (Titles in **bold** denote the first mention of a work shown in the current exhibition.)

sculp-metal   *Sculpture was a separate thing, as was the easel picture, but it did not require a wall like a picture. It did not even need a roof. It was an object that could exist for itself alone, and it was well to give it entirely the character of a complete thing about which one could walk, and which one could look at from all sides. And yet it had to distinguish itself somehow from other things, the ordinary things which everyone could touch. It had to become unimpeachable, sacrosanct, separated from chance and time, through which it rose isolated and miraculous, like the face of a seer. It had to be given its own certain place, in which no arbitrariness had placed it, and it must be intercalated in the silent continuance of space and its great laws. It had to be fitted into the space that surrounded it, as into a niche; its certainty, steadiness and loftiness did not spring from its significance but from its harmonious adjustment to its environment.*

Rainer Maria Rilke, *Rodin*, 1903[29]

I had this image of a flashlight in my head and I wanted to go and buy one as a model. I looked for a week for what I thought looked like an ordinary flashlight, and I found all kinds of flashlights with red plastic shields, wings on the sides, all kinds of things, and I finally found one that I wanted. And it made me very suspicious of my idea, because it was so difficult to find this thing I had thought was so common.

Jasper Johns to David Sylvester, 1965[30]

Jasper Johns groups together, and silvers over, flashlights and electric bulbs, symbolizing light unless one chooses to see a more obvious symbolical meaning.

Stuart Preston, 1959[31]

• sculp-metal IT MODELS LIKE CLAY — HARDENS INTO METAL!

After *Flag* Johns turned his attention to other man-made 'things the mind already knows' that could be appropriated to painting in such a way that they would remain what they were to an extent that the resulting object would effect an oscillation between its character as sign and referent. These 'ordinary things' tended to be, like the Stars and Stripes, flat things, whole entities or complete systems that gave whatever Johns made of them their design, dimensions and non-hierarchic character. In 1955 the first of these things, the individual numbers 1, 2, 5, and 7, made not in the same way but with the same materials as *Flag*, paint, wax and newsprint scrap, became *Figure 1*, *Figure 2*, *Figure 5*, and *Figure 7*. The question 'Is it a painting, or is it a flag?' was turned into 'Is it a painting, or is it a 7?' In 1956 Johns tried to effect the same kind of hermeneutic intrigue with the alphabet. He took an alphabet chart that he had seen in a book and used it as the basis for *Gray Alphabets* (The Menil Collection, Houston). The chart provided him with a closed and complete system like the designs of the flag and target. The next year he used it to make *Gray Numbers* (Collection of Kimiko and John Powers).

As well as using these flat things, Johns also used three dimensional things and bits of three-dimensional things to make paintings. *Book* (Martin Z. Margulies Collection, Miami) and *Drawer* (Rose Art Museum, Brandeis University, Waltham), both made in 1957, provide us with examples. The objects that give their names as titles to these works also determine their shapes and/or dimensions in more or less the same way that the Stars and Stripes set the shape and proportions of *Flag*. Steinberg, recalling how Apollinaire had 'predicted a greater role in modern art for the real object, which he called the picture's "internal frame" ', pointed out how the surface of these objects 'is not contained by an external frame, but is retained from within'.[32] The shape and dimension of each object is an 'internal frame' that 'serves… to diminish the margin of choice' and reduce 'the arbitrariness of where the picture ends'.[33] The drawer front, with its two handles, fixes the width of the canvas used to make *Drawer*. The book, open to show the full double-spread of its pages, fixes *Book*'s width and height. The drawer both makes and destroys the integrity of the canvas. Dabs of grey pigmented wax busy their way all-over the surface. (This time there's no newsprint scrap.) The book comes in place of a canvas and stretcher. Like the front of the drawer, it is also covered with dabbed strokes of pigmented wax: red for the open pages, yellow for their edges, and blue for the binding. Solomon, in his catalogue essay for the 1964 Johns retrospective, responded to these works in much the same way that he had responded to *Flag*. His view was that here, as there, Johns 'confronts us with a series of unanswerable enigmatic questions: What is real and what is paint? What "is" and what is "made"? What is hidden from us on the front of the canvas, and on the obscured surface beneath? Have we been told everything, or is there more?'[34] Ten years later, Max Kozloff referred to *Book* as a 'painting' but immediately checked himself to ask '– or is it a sculpture?'.[35]

In these works Johns was turning a trick on the avant-garde's concern with, and resistance to, aspects and objects of mass culture. It was a good trick. He was using 'ordinary things' – already existing manufactured things – as resources, appropriating them to his art as signs and structures but in a way that neither celebrated nor criticised them but simultaneously celebrated and set up a critical resistance to them or to their incorporation in art. The meaning and value of the Stars and Stripes was neither affirmed nor denied but both affirmed and denied. A similar undecidable effect was achieved with numbers and letters, and a drawer and a book. It seems to me that the value of the trick might have to be seen and understood as the uncertainty it effects in the beholder, an uncertainty about his or her identity, and about the identity of 'things', that he or she usually refuses to acknowledge. In other words, it is a re-presentation of an uncertainty that is determined, in part at least and however mediated, by the motor force that determines the kind of society that produces and is enamoured of mass culture.

What I have been trying to do is build a framework for seeing and explaining Johns' sculpture. There is a matrix here also, one that Johns would have taken stock of and worked out of in 1958, the year he began to make work as a 'sculptor' rather than as a 'painter'. January–February 1958 was the moment of his first one-man show at the Castelli Gallery. This show displayed a representative selection of work including *Flag*, *Target with Plaster Casts*, *Figure 7*, *Book* and *Drawer*, and gave Johns cause for retrospection and retrodiction about his intentions and ambitions as an artist. Perhaps he took up sculpture to clarify those intentions and ambitions. Johns' first sculptures seem to have had a mainly private purpose. Perhaps he wanted to have a rest from painting where he had done all he could for the time being. It seems likely that just as he had 'been thinking about painting and what made a painting a painting', he would also have been thinking about 'what made a sculpture a sculpture'. Since many of his paintings 'played with three-dimensional aspects', he might have been curious about the relation between painting and sculpture, and about what, if the objects he had made were paintings, would fulfil his expectations of sculpture.[36]

Johns' first sculpture came out of his pictorial art. In 1957 he made a drawing in pencil and wash on paper of a light bulb suspended by a flex from a ceiling fitting.[37] He tried to make the subject of this drawing in plaster, but the resulting object was too fragile and it broke.[38] Though the drawing was later successfully made into a lithograph and a lead relief, the hanging light bulb was never taken into three-dimensions. Johns seems to have come to the decision that it was a subject best suited to two-dimensions. Mindful of this failed sculpture and the kinds of sculptures Johns made around or because of it, we can assume that when he began making sculpture he was committed to two key aspects of modernist practice. He was committed to an insistence on volume and shape – magnitude in three-dimensions – as a fundamental condition of sculpture. And he was committed to an insistence on sculpture's concreteness as, what Rilke called, a 'complete' or 'separate thing', a special kind of thing that would distinguish itself from 'ordinary things'. However – and not surprisingly given the beginning established by *Flag* – as much as Johns was committed to insisting on volume and shape and the 'separate thing-ness' of sculpture, he was also concerned to simultaneously question and problematise volume and shape and 'separate thing-ness' in the works he made as a sculptor. For the 1957 drawing to become a sculpture, Johns had get rid of the ceiling, the ceiling fitting and as much flex as was possible in order to concentrate on the volume and shape of the 'ordinary thing' – the light bulb – as a 'separate thing'.

According to the modern tradition in sculpture, the sculptor had to create or originate volume and shape by handling material according to, or by staying true to, its characteristics: carving it, modelling it or constructing with it. What he made had not existed before he brought it into being, and it identified and offered an innate category of experience. As we have seen, Johns' practice was to appropriate commonplace, conventional 'ordinary things', and measure and transfer them to canvas as a base on which to work. The flag of the United States of America, the numbers and the alphabet, the drawer and the book did not originate in him. As with the structures, proportions and dimensions of his paintings, so with the volumes and shapes of his sculptures. Faced with the need to originate volume and shape, he copied them exactly or cast them from things that were coherent and closed, seemingly impersonal and classless. What was fundamental to modern sculpture's identity as a 'separate thing', an original volume and shape and experience, was in the case of Johns' sculptures already made and well known as the volume and shape and experience of an 'ordinary thing'.

The first objects that Johns made as a sculptor were based on a light bulb and a flashlight. *Light Bulb I* and *Light Bulb II* are both made of sculp-metal – about which I will have something to say in a moment – but Johns does not remember how they were made. It is quite likely that *Light Bulb I* was made in two pieces by building up layers of sculp-metal against the side of a negative mould.[39] Whereas *Light Bulb I* and *Light Bulb II* approximate the weight of actual light bulbs,[40] the later light bulb sculptures, *Light Bulb* (1960)[41] and *Bronze* (1960–1961) were made in bronze from plaster casts and are very heavy. For *Flashlight I* Johns took an actual flashlight and covered it with sculp-metal – a bronze version of this was made in 1960: *Flashlight*.[42] *Flashlight II* is made of thick papier mâché of the kind that can be bought ready made for pressing into moulds. *Flashlight III* is made of plaster; its flashlight perhaps taken from the same mould as that used for *Flashlight II*. A bronze cast of *Flashlight III* was made in 1987. Although it must have been technically difficult, in each case Johns has managed to incorporate the glass that protects the flashlight's bulb and reflector.

Formally, when made in sculp-metal or cast in papier mâché, plaster or bronze, the light bulbs and flashlights that give their volume and shape to Johns' objects work very well as modern sculptures. They hold some characteristics in common with certain works by, for example, Brancusi and Matisse. And they occupy space in much the same way. Brancusi's *Sleeping Muse* and *Prometheus*, *The First Cry* and *The Newborn* come to mind immediately; Matisse's *Head of Jeannette II* and *Reclining Nude III* less immediately. Like these sculptures, each of Johns' light bulb sculptures qua light bulb has the form of an enclosed and contained unit. It is at rest but has a rotational movement along its horizontal axis that is keyed visually by the screw-thread at its light bulb 'base' which then balloons to make the 'bulb'. It can support itself where the curved surface of its 'bulb' touches whatever surface it is placed on, but it is unstable in relation to other objects and will roll unless provided with a base. Although the flashlight is a cylinder, not a bulb, it, too, has a marked rotation around a horizontal axis; this is keyed by the grooves that travel around its head unit and around both ends of the horizontal ribbing that runs along its battery case. Like the light bulb, it can support itself but will roll without a base. Only **Light Bulb II** is excused a base. It is here that Matisse's *Reclining Nude III* of 1929 (The Baltimore Museum of Art) comes to mind where, it has been observed, 'the pose of the figure forms an enclosed and contained unit; it can support itself without a base; the recumbent posture allows for a maximum of invention and distortion of shape without anatomical or structural consequences. Although the figure is at rest, there is a tremendous rotational movement inside the body… the forms of the thighs and lower abdomen are transformed as if into twisted strands of rope'.[43] It seems to me that Johns' *Light Bulb II* shares certain distinctive characteristics with this conventional modern sculpture. No more than that. It has a contained overall shape; an extended looping that returns and keeps its movement within the object; and a means of support that is integral to and of its form. *Light Bulb II* rests on the light bulb's switch mechanism and/or on the two twisted wires coming out of it, which bend at a right angle away from it, and then bend again, and again, before returning their direction to the 'bulb'. The point is not that *Light Bulb II* is anthropomorphic. Like an actual light bulb, it rests easily in the hand, and invites this response – I've read that 'when we hold the bulb it becomes a sensual, even erotic, organic shape' – but it isn't anthropomorphic.[44] We don't see and understand its bulb as a torso or its twisted flex as extended limbs. As an object it is too small to evoke the human figure, or any specific part of it, and lacks the necessary axis of focus or interpellation that anthropomorphism seems to demand. Anthropomorphism results when the artist takes his sculpture for a person, consciously or unconsciously makes it *that*, and in such a way that it presents itself to the beholder as *that*. The work then confronts the beholder *as if* it were a person. Things don't do that. A light bulb neither confronts nor presents itself to us. It does not have limbs or a front or a back. Nor has Johns' sculpture. A flashlight has a front and a back but we do not look at Johns' sculpture of a flashlight as we look at a flashlight. In fact, we rarely look at a flashlight. When we use one, we look down its battery case, out over its head unit and down its beam of light. We look away from it. Johns' sculpture disrupts this axis of focus, flummoxes us with regard to its and our best point of view. With the exception perhaps, of **Bronze** (light bulb, socket and wire on grid), where the syntagmatic arrangement of parts was contingent on their not being able to be fitted together into a unitary object and so disposed according to Johns' sense of the style and structure of a light bulb,[45] we are presented with no particular place or places from which to view these sculptures. Nor are we given anything that might encourage us to see and understand them as other than what they are. The point is that all these sculptures are too emphatically or literally *of* a light bulb or *of* a flashlight – which is not to say that that is all they are *of* – to affect us as something else. In part, at least, that is why, with the exception of *Light Bulb II*, resting on its own terms in the condition of sculpture, each one needs the support of a base.

Towards the end of his essay in the catalogue of the 1964 Jewish Museum retrospective, Solomon turned to a discussion of the sculptures. Brief though it is, this was probably the first serious discussion of Johns' work as a sculptor. Not surprisingly, for it was Solomon who had asked 'Is it a painting, or is it a flag?', he pointed out how the likeness of the sculptures, compared with the real objects, creates a 'genuine confusion' about their identity. 'The ambiguity in his sculptures,' he wrote, 'is overwhelming.'[46] He then went on to point out that when we look at Johns' light bulbs and flashlights 'we encounter a perplexing uncertainty over whether or not he has simply cast the real objects in Sculp-metal or bronze, or even just coated them with Sculp-metal, since they appear so true to life… The result is that these pieces give the effect of objects trying to be sculpture, and we are thrown back into that now familiar realm of ambiguity'.[47]

Because Johns' sculptures of light bulbs and flashlights are small, fragile, modest in appearance, different in meaning and value from 'ordinary things' but quite like them, they needed to be secured and set apart from them. Putting a sculpture on a base, placing it away from, but in relation to, other things, and the beholder, emphasises its identity as a 'separate thing'. The base declares the object it supports to be different from other things, and different from other sculptures. However, the bases that Johns made for his sculptures do not function straightforwardly in the ways that bases are usually made to function. *Light Bulb I*, for example, is, at first sight, almost indistinguishable from its base. Separated, the base seems much more sculptural than the sculpture it supports. That is to say, the bases do not so much set and mark off as special the volumes and shapes they support as assert their own volumes and shapes as special. They, and not the sculptures, are what seem to have the invented, original volumes and shapes that are taken as essential to the modern condition of sculpture. The bases set off what they support as different from 'ordinary things' but not necessarily different as sculptures. Rather than remove the sculptures from that 'realm of ambiguity', the bases contribute to their ambiguity and the uncertainty they effect in the beholder.

Consider, for example, *Flashlight II*, where both the sculpture and the base have been made of papier mâché, but in different ways. The sculpture was cast in two pieces from a mould taken from a flashlight. The pieces were then joined together; their meeting disguised, and the surface of the whole thing worked on, filled in and built-up in places, pressed and smoothed down in others, the circular grooves round the head unit made sharper and the ribbing along the battery case interrupted and distressed. The base does not have such a surface, or not one that was added afterwards. Its volume and surface came together at the same time as Johns worked the papier mâché into a rough oblong slab, using his thumb, index and middle fingers, to pinch, push and press it into shape. The beholder can fit his or her fingers into the indentations and hollows and imagine the process that made the base what it is. The papier mâché cracked as it dried – the fissures haven't been filled in – and in some places gobs of it have failed to adhere completely to the mass. The base was made in a manner quite at odds with how the sculpture was made. The base undulates, and is lumpy; it is much less balanced and contained than the flashlight. Johns affirmed the material characteristics of the papier mâché to an extent that he avoided in the process used to make the sculpture. Here he was concerned to attend to the softness, relative inertness, and passivity of the papier mâché, modelling it with a directness that has to do with the experience of volume. In this sense, the base is much more conventionally 'sculptural' than the sculpture it supports.

Though it is not so obviously stated, the same relation between the sculpture and its base is there in *Flashlight III*. Max Kozloff, probably the first person to write at length about it, saw *Flashlight III* as 'sinking into frothy plaster' and 'decomposing (or possibly emerging from) inchoate matter' and 'deliquescing in a substance'.[48] Roberta Bernstein saw it as 'emerging from formless matter'.[49] To my eye it neither sinks, decomposes, melts nor emerges. About that Kozloff and Bernstein were wrong, but they were correct in trying to write of the near-unity that the flashlight and its base effect, a near-unity that is sculptural, and traditionally so. Kozloff was also correct when he remarked, apropos of *Flashlight III*, that the 'density and texture' and the 'thingness of sculpture' – the 'separate thingness' – was something that Johns wanted to transcend in his sculpture.[50] Partially correct, that is. Johns did not want to transcend the 'thingness of sculpture' in his sculptures. To have done so would have put what he made beyond the condition of sculpture. He did not want to do that. 'But I *am* a sculptor, am I not?' As I wrote a moment ago, he wanted to work with and against the 'thingness' of sculpture. He wanted to achieve it in his sculptures but simultaneously problematise it or deny it. That play on 'thingness', density and texture in Kozloff's terms, and its problematisation or denial, is evident in *Flashlight III* in the relation of the sculpture to its base. Only here, the density and texture and the problematisation or denial of it are brought so close together that the difference is easily missed. Looking closely helps.

The base of *Flashlight III* seems to have been made out of several bits and pieces. At the top there may be an oblong block, a little wider and longer than the sculpture it is there to support, and this, in turn, might be supported by at least one other thing. The internal structure was tied together, supported or strengthened, with wire snipped from a wire coat-hanger. And this was then covered with dollops of plaster that were smoothed and shaped by various instruments, including the fingers, while the plaster was wet or drying. At several places, the coat-hanger wire breaks through the plaster. Once it was dry, some of the plaster was chiselled away to make a vertical surface where the base meets whatever it is placed on. The chisel worked across the surface, in some places diagonally but mostly vertically, gouging and prizing away chunks of plaster from the mass. The base, then, was made by modelling and carving. It raises the sculpture on a structure that resulted from a process of horizontal layering, stacking and plastering. But that obvious effect of structural horizontality is contradicted by the vertical scars left by the chisel as it pressed down on, through and out of the plaster. Somewhere in the process of building up and demolishing, adding and subtracting, the flashlight, more or less complete, was put in place, and plaster was built up along its sides, head unit and battery case, and smoothed to meet it, to stick and hold it there. This was done in such a way that it did not spoil the effect of the flashlight as a 'separate thing'. The flashlight is neither sinking into nor emerging from the base. It is gripped by it as a thing that is different. When everything was dry, the flashlight and its base were rubbed with oil which changed the texture and colour and unified the different kinds of plaster and plaster work that had gone into its making. However, on examination, the unity of the object gives way to reveal the same set of problematised relations, evidenced in *Light Bulb I* and *Flashlight II*, between a 'thing' and a 'separate thing', and a base and a sculpture.[51]

And so to *Flashlight I* where the sculpture and its base are kept apart. As I mentioned in passing earlier, here the flashlight is an actual flashlight that has been covered with sculp-metal. The base is a block of wood that has also been covered with sculp-metal. I have been writing around the surfaces of Johns' first sculptures for a while now, usually only commenting that the casts had been 'worked on', but here the surface quality of the sculpture and its effects are so clearly staged that they are almost impossible to avoid or ignore.

Sculp-metal. The advertisement was an ever-present in *Art News* during the 1950s. It was usually placed in one of the side columns of the section devoted to small ads and 'new sources, new materials'. It always featured a photograph of a small sculp-metal bust of a child – it is difficult to know whether it is a boy or a girl – with a pudding-basin hair-cut. By 1954 the copy had become standardised to read: 'The new creative medium! • sculp-metal. It models like clay – Hardens into metal! 1001 uses in Arts and Crafts. Send 10c for handbook "working in sculp-metal". Sculp-metal is applied with palette knife or fingers. Pieces air harden; burnish to rich aluminum'. The advertisement was aimed at amateur artists and modellers. Forty years on, sculp-metal is still stocked by the art-supplies shops around Canal Street, New York. People have been buying it. Not only Johns.

Sculp-metal is a specious stuff, a complex mixture of tints, fillers, vinyl resin, aluminium powder, toluol and methyl ethyl ketone, that comes ready to use from the can. It has the consistency and texture of pizza-dough and can be applied with a spatula or a palette knife or with the fingers. Used in this way, it can be built up in successive layers to a mass. It can also be mixed with special thinners to various consistencies. Thinned, it can be used like oil paint and even sprayed. Sculp-metal dries quickly to a light matt grey, and can be smoothed with emery cloth, in which case it stays matt, or it can be burnished with a metal file or wire wool, in which case it takes on either a low or high lustre finish, according to the advertisement, like 'rich aluminum'. If a 'high, mirror-like finish' is required, you have to burnish the sculp-metal with the back of a teaspoon.[52]

Johns covered the flashlight with sculp-metal. While the flashlight is textured, the bulb and the reflector are smooth (have they been painted with sculp-metal, or aluminium paint?). The flashlight's 'rich aluminum' – I'd say it was 'dull' rather than 'rich' – was achieved with several separate applications of sculp-metal, each application following the direction of the horizontal ribbing on the battery case and the grooves around the head unit. Here and there, several applications have been built up to obscure the ribs and grooves. In other places, the sculp-metal has been layered and then smoothed. The process developed here set the pattern for the way Johns worked on the surfaces of the casts used for *Flashlight II* and *Flashlight III*, transferring and adapting it from sculp-metal to papier mâché and plaster. Looking at *Flashlight I*, however, it becomes clearer than when we looked at *Flashlight II* and *Flashlight III* that what we are looking at is a surface that has been added to another surface, a surface that asserts and denies what it has come in place of. At first, the sculpture looks as if it is made of aluminium. On closer inspection, it becomes apparent that what we are looking at cannot be metal: it is not metallic, but metal-like; and everywhere there are signs of handling and touch, unmediated by any casting process, that effect not the density of metal but the cutaneous quality of painting. It is not, as Stuart Preston thought, a 'silvered flashlight' but a flashlight covered with something metal-like that retains all the directness and personality of the artist's touch.[53] Not just a 'thing' but a flashlight that seems to have been turned into a 'separate thing'. But if it is that, as a sculpture, its magnitude in three-dimensions, mass, density and texture are contradicted or denied by the effect of the sculp-metal which covers its volume and shape as a modernist painting covers a flat surface.

As to the base, there is a density there that results from the thickness of the sculp-metal and from the fact that it is covering a block of wood. There are signs to this effect. The sculp-metal has been almost trowelled on, and, in places, where its application has exceeded the maker's recommended $1/8$" layer, it has dried to a wrinkle that has had to be smoothed over. Generally, its application has followed the grain of the wood, and in at least one place it has gone over and filled in a knot. It is a conventional base, albeit one covered with an unconventional material. Whatever mass and density it has, it dramatises the sculpture's effected lack of mass and density – a lack playfully affirmed by the two thin wires that support the actual weight of the flashlight.

Handling and touch. It has been said, correctly, that 'Johns' art operates in the mode of touch, continually reorienting whatever localised physical connection to his works the viewer may succeed in establishing'.[54] His sculptures and paintings 'have parts that relate to one another in conflicting and overdetermined ways' and 'seem to demonstrate that their representational meaning will change according to the conditions of their close inspection'.[55] When the beholder closely inspects Johns' sculptures, he or she becomes involved in a process of seeing and understanding a tactile order that is *of* the sculptures and *of* Johns and *of* him or her. Since the physicality registered in and by the handling and touching is a common one, constructed and lived, it can be, and has been, given a range of adjectives that try to characterise its effects. Something is being tried for in the surfaces of Johns' sculptures: a personal touch that provides Johns and us with an experience of an authoring subjectivity, a controlling presence, physical and mental.

As Johns used it, straight from the can or thinned, applied with a knife, fingers or a brush, sculp-metal provided him with a metal-like substitute for wax and newsprint scrap. You only have to look at the sculp-metal and collage *Flag* that he made in 1960 to see how, if he wanted to, he could use sculp-metal to produce a surface like that of the first *Flag* – notice how the postage stamp and the bit of newsprint scrap at the right of the lowest stripes (ordinary things that contribute to the meaning of this particular Stars and Stripes) have been, respectively, stuck and painted into place with sculp-metal.[56] When the first commentators on Johns' art tried to describe his handling and touch, they did so with reference to Abstract Expressionism which was then becoming firmly established as 'The New American Painting'.[57] Each day Johns and the other ambitious avant-garde artists who desired a productive novelty for their work had to make relations with Abstract Expressionism and differ their art from it.[58] The surfaces of Johns' paintings seemed to evidence a relation with it but they were not amenable to description in the same terms. In a moment, I will have more to say about the metaphorics and performance of masculinity. Here all that needs to be pointed out is that Johns avoided the metaphorics and performance of masculinity that were so much part of Abstract Expressionism's way of possessing and using the surface.[59] But he disavowed them from within the space of modernist practice occupied by the Abstract Expressionists. Johns' handling and touch, his characteristic gesture, was different, and commentators had to find new terms for it. Here is an incomplete listing of what they came up with: caressing and gentle; delicate and refined; fastidious; fussy; patient; intimate; sensual and sensuous. The commentators were trying to say something that was difficult to say, and on the whole I think they said it very well. Accumulated like that, for the sake of speed, the terms seem to have connotations of femininity, but they do not secure Johns' handling and touch as feminine. The writing on Johns' touch veered towards characterising it as feminine but something prevented it from being securely gendered in the feminine. Maybe John's touch has to be seen and understood as sexualised in a way that cannot be resolved in terms of either masculine or feminine touching.[60]

I am concerned with seeing and understanding the handling and touch that put the sculp-metal on the flashlight to make *Flashlight I*. The same touch can be recognised on the surface of *Flashlight II* and *Flashlight III*. It is characteristically *of* Johns. Handling and touch are like handwriting. Johns' touch began on the surface of *Flag*. Here the volume and shape provided by the flashlight comes in place of the flatness of the fabric. But the touch is the same and it effects a similar feeling of physical and mental intimacy. The adjectives that were first used to situate Johns' touch in relation to Abstract Expressionism still apply. As on the surface of *Flag*, Johns' touch on the surface of *Flashlight I* might also be seen as marking a disavowal of the same visual metaphors. The adjectives used to describe Johns' touch tracked a disavowal in the masculine. But not a complete disavowal. Nor could it be. The disavowal does not abolish masculinity. It recognises it as a limit to be dealt with. Masculinity is there in Johns' touch, not as a securely established self but as a disavowed self. The sculp-metal surface of *Flashlight I*, uncertainly metallic and painting, like the surface of *Flag*, certainly neither painting nor collage but painting and collage, can be thought of as a space for the situation of another identity, one that could never be completely achieved. Never completely negated, the disavowed masculine metaphorics of touch remains residual in this space marking the possibility of an avowed other kind of touch that has to be understood as, or associated with, a kind of non-masculine masculinity.

Johns distinguishes his sculptures from 'ordinary things which everyone could touch' by giving them another surface and another tactility but in a way that does not make them thoroughly 'unimpeachable' as 'separate things' that can be seen as sculptures. Their cutaneous effect is like that of painting, but not that of 'The New American Painting' or Abstract Expressionism. Having decided to make sculptures, Johns made 'separate things' that problematised their separateness from the 'ordinary things' they came in place of and, in some cases, their difference from paintings also. In doing this, they also problematised the beholder's relation to them. Although each sculpture made in 1958 has its own 'certain place', that place is also uncertain. Rather than 'certainty', 'steadiness', 'loftiness', and 'harmonious adjustment to the environment', each sculpture effects uncertainty, instability, and a basic disharmony. Johns' sculpture matches Rilke's description and resists or denies it. This is an aspect of the hermeneutic intrigue that began with *Flag*.

Further to the emphasis on surface and touch and the way it works with and against the sculptural subject of volume and shape, density and texture, and 'thingness', that I have approached mainly through a discussion of *Flashlight I* and sculp-metal, it seems clear that there are other concerns that ought to be mentioned. The concern with light is obvious. Can you see a 'more obvious symbolical meaning'? Not so obvious, perhaps, is the concern with covering and concealing as a mode of revealing, with not seeing and seeing. What caused Johns to be interested in these themes is not my concern here. Suffice it to say, they were some of the concerns and themes that were established in Johns' art in 1954 when he first got interested in making plaster casts of body parts. Another beginning.

Painted Bronze   *The idea for the ale cans was like a present. I felt I should already have known to do it as a sculpture: it had the right scale, it was already there — all I had to do was look over and see it, and then do it. Doing the ale cans made me see other things around me, so I did the Savarin Can.*

                          Jasper Johns to Michael Crichton, 1977[61]

            ...in the big Savarin *print, which began because a poster was needed for my show at the Whitney Museum, I drew one of my sculptures much larger than life; but that was a deliberate attempt at advertising on my part.*

                          Jasper Johns to Christian Geelhaar, 1978[62]

Like *Flag*, and several other important works by Johns, **Painted Bronze** (ale cans) has a pretext. Here is the story Johns tells about it. 'I was doing at the time sculptures of small objects – flashlights and light bulbs. Then I heard a story about Willem de Kooning. He was annoyed with my dealer, Leo Castelli, for some reason and said something like, "That son-of-a-bitch you could give him two beer cans and he could sell them." I heard this and thought, "What a sculpture – two beer cans." It seemed to fit in perfectly with what I was doing, so I did them – and Leo sold them.'[63]

Painted Bronze : two cans of Ballantine Ale were cast in plaster; a base was modelled to put them on; it was thumb printed; and everything was cast in bronze. The labels were then painted onto the cans. The smaller can has been opened; there is a three-ring trade mark on its top; it is a Southern can from Florida. The larger can has been left unopened; its top lacks the three-ring sign; it is a Northern can from New York. One is heavy; the other is not so heavy. And so on. This is fascinating stuff and there is delight to be taken in it, but more important for under-standing what *Painted Bronze* might mean is the fact that its beginnings were in a remark made by de Kooning about Castelli. Here I need to resume my earlier discussion of Abstract Expressionism and the metaphorics and performance of masculinity. De Kooning was, in 1960, the most important action painting Abstract Expressionist. Johns' dealer did not sell Abstract Expressionism – indeed, his gallery was set up to market something else.[64] *Painted Bronze* is a sculpture that comments on an individual artist, his ideas about art and his attitude to the art market, and on the whole ethos of Abstract Expressionism. De Kooning's work, specifically, and Abstract Expressionism, generally, were resources available to Johns but there was a lot in them that he could not use and did not want.[65] As we saw a moment ago, he was, for example, not interested in appropriating the metaphorics of masculinity that were an essential part of a lot of Abstract Expressionist painting or the performance of masculinity that went into its supposedly 'stubborn, difficult, even desperate effort to discover the self'.[66] Abstract Expressionism involved, in one way or another, the dramatisation of the exposure of feeling – 'an effort to which the whole personality should be recklessly committed,' as one critic put it – and for some artists, like de Kooning, that also meant living an aggressively heterosexual life and getting drunk both in and out of the Cedar Street Tavern, a favourite bar of the Abstract Expressionists and their cronies.[67] By picking up de Kooning's jibe about

Castelli and using it to make a sculpture, Johns continued to differ himself and his practice from Abstract Expressionism.

What painting there is on *Painted Bronze* (ale cans) is confined to the labels. In so far as it does not effect a maximum presence as a painted surface, it is not obviously modernist painting. But it is punctilious painting. This is the label that Kozloff saw Johns copying as if it was a 'life' model.[68] Nor is it obviously expressionist painting: a personality may well have been committed to the task of making it, but certainly not 'recklessly'. We are not supposed to see it as an 'exposure of feeling'. And though Johns was drinking beer at the time; there is nothing in *Painted Bronze* that could be taken as signifying that he was reckless in his drinking habits. Of course, he may have been, but then one of the cans remains unopened. Someone who got close to him tells us that 'Johns used Ballantine Ale cans, most likely because the brand was a personal favourite'. She also points out that 'the simplicity of the can's label design and its bronze colour' made it a suitable model.[69] (The colour and patina of the bronze will have dulled with time.) I wonder what de Kooning's favourite brand was? Different communities have different drinking habits and prefer different bars and brands. Habits, places and labels signify 'mythologies'. Johns avoided the Cedar Street Tavern and liked Ballantine Ale.

Painted Bronze (ale cans): Johns takes over a story about something de Kooning said, uses it to make a joke at de Kooning's expense, and ends up with a twice-told tale about expression and masculine identity. However, seeing and understanding *Painted Bronze* in this way is to position Johns and his sculpture in a knowing relation of association with an Abstract Expressionist painter and painting. We can also position Johns in relation to a sculptor who was associated with some of the Abstract Expressionists, and by doing so differ and defer his sculpture from the metaphorics of masculinity that were so much part of sculpture and being a sculptor in New York during the late 1950s and early 1960s. The sculptor I have in mind is David Smith.

Robert Motherwell's recollections of Smith give us a complex bachelor machismo, a person who would arrive unexpectedly with half a young bear he had shot and a need to drink any companion under the table.[70] Motherwell lists the 'male things' that Smith liked talking about: 'Mercedes-Benz..., shot guns, the wonders of Dunhill's tobacco shop, where the best dark bread and sweet butter was, baroque music, Scotch tweeds, the pleasures and mysteries of Europe, the Plaza over the Chelsea Hotel…, the reminiscences of a Western American youth between the two world wars, in short, his whole "Ernest Hemmingway" side…'.[71] The performance of masculinity that went into the making of his constructed and built sculptures is represented in nearly every photograph of him taken at Bolton Landing and Voltri, and I need not labour its description. Smith helmeted, visored or goggled; gloved and leather-aproned; moving metal plates into place with block and chain tackle; feet firmly on the ground and sometimes unbalanced (no lithe athleticism here). There's no doubt about Smith's masculinity, or his performance of it. It was factory production, heavy work that took great physical effort and also a kind of masculine camaraderie. Which is not to say that the sculptures were the result of just that. According to Motherwell, Smith was a mixture of Vivaldi and a Mack truck, and occasionally a Vivaldi-like delicacy of touch was caught in the photographs, as when, for example, a heavily armoured toe tenderly taps a bit of *Voltri Bolton X* into place on the factory floor.[72] Faced with the anthropomorphic power of the sculptures, however, it is easy to overlook the delicacy that was part of their manufacture and that makes them what they are.

In 1964 Smith was interviewed by Frank O'Hara for *Art: New York*, an educational television series. O'Hara commented that the works arranged in the sculpture parks at Bolton Landing looked like men and women at a cocktail party. Smith corrected him: 'Well, they're all girl sculptures… I don't make boy sculptures'.[73] On one level, this remark asserts Smith's heterosexuality over and against O'Hara's homosexuality. Smith didn't make 'boys'. On another level, it is merely a blunt statement of a bit of modernist art ideology: the performance of masculinity determines work that is focussed on the female body and the expression of femaleness. Demoiselles; big nudes and blue nudes; weeping women and girls before mirrors; Ledas and princesses; virgins and brides stripped bare by bachelors, even; Woman; etc. Smith saw his sculptures as 'girls'. In that sense they were part of the modernist tradition. On yet another level, the remark can be taken in a more private or familial way. In the last ten years of his life, as O'Hara would have known, Smith inscribed several of his sculptures with the names of his daughters, Rebecca and Candida. Some of his sculptures were dedicated to or were evocative of his daughters. Motherwell recollected Smith's affection for his daughters. And he also noted that he was 'mad about very young women'.[74] Whatever 'girls' Smith saw his sculptures as, his daughters or other 'young women', the point is that O'Hara saw them differently. While Smith saw them as gendered in the feminine, O'Hara saw them as gendered as male and female. What was, for Smith, secure and stable as feminine was, for O'Hara, both masculine and feminine. Smith, in conversation with O'Hara, and aware of his sexuality, asserts their femininity.

The practice of modernist sculpture seems to entail, as it does for modernist painting, the performance of masculinity and a belief in the security and stability of a metaphorics of masculinity in the work of art. Both the performance and the metaphors are, however, unstable and ambivalent: the toe taps tenderly in the work boot, and the art can be seen as either masculine or feminine. Works of art can only be seen and understood as stable and certain in the assertion of ideology. Johns, it seems, wanted to ensure that his work would not be taken as having been produced by a conventional performance of masculinity, and made his art in a relation of difference with regard to the dominant masculinist modes of painting and sculpture. The choice of sculp-metal as the medium of his first sculptures has to be understood as an aspect of that rejection or denial. Sculp-metal was an amateur's medium; it wasn't – and still isn't – on the avant-garde's list of suitable degenerate or trivial materials. It is an ersatz metal that Johns used not as if it was metal but as if it was paint. Using it that way, he was able to situate what he made with it in a relation of difference from the usual ways that advanced painters and sculptors used paint and metal. De Kooning's comment about Castelli and beer cans gave Johns the pretext with which to perform another differencing movement based on cast bronze, a medium that was rarely used by avant-garde sculptors in New York. Traditional and out of favour in relation to the constructed sculpture of Smith and others, cast bronze might have had a value, like sculp-metal, as a daft material with which to make serious avant-garde sculpture that was different from usual avant-garde sculpture. The works of art that Johns made could neither be thoroughly or securely celebrated nor criticised in discourse with the usual metaphors. Their difference was partly determined by the performance of a non-masculine masculinity, and their effect was, and still is, an assertion of the instability and uncertainty of sexuality and things.

> *I am concerned with a thing's not being what it was, with its becoming something other than what it is, with any moment in which one identifies a thing precisely and with the slipping away of that moment, with at any moment seeing or saying and letting it go at that.*
>
> Jasper Johns to G. R. Swenson, 1964[75]

…we look in a certain direction and we see one thing, we look in another way and we see another thing. So that what we call 'thing' becomes very elusive and very flexible, and it involves the arrangement of elements before us, and it also involves the arrangement of our senses at the time of encountering this thing. It involves the way we focus, what we are willing to accept as being there.

Jasper Johns to David Sylvester, 1965[76]

One thing working one way
Another thing working another way.
One thing working different ways
at different times.

Jasper Johns, *Sketchbook* [1965][77]

…my work is in part concerned with the possibility of things being taken for one thing or another – with questionable areas of identification and usage and procedure – with thought rather than secure things.

Jasper Johns to Vivien Raynor, 1973[78]

De Kooning's comment about Castelli and Johns' allegory of it, *Painted Bronze* (ale cans), were then displaced onto **Painted Bronze** (Savarin can with brushes), an object that supplemented them with an obvious reference to painting. *Painted Bronze* (Savarin can with brushes) is a sculpture about painting. Johns took a Savarin coffee can which he had been using in the studio to hold turpentine and paintbrushes and translated it and its contents into plaster. The plaster version was sent to the foundry and cast in bronze. The bronze components were then cleansed and chased. There must be at least eighteen individual elements in its coming to be what it is: the can and the now metal turpentine in the can, and the seventeen paintbrushes. Assembled and painted, it was then titled *Painted Bronze* though sometimes, and increasingly after its appearance at the Johns retrospective at the Whitney Museum of American Art in 1977, a parenthesis is added to make it *Painted Bronze (Savarin)*.

Painted Bronze (Savarin can with brushes) has been referred to as a replica, but it isn't. The details of the label, for example, have been copied but not exactly. The brushes, as one commentator put it, 'seem so perfect that it is hard to believe that they are not the originals, even on close examination'.[79] But it is the very perfection of their painting as painting that proves the lie of them. It has also been described as a trompe l'oeil work where it would have to function in a kind of game that the beholder plays by being deceived, but Johns is surely not playing that kind of game or not playing it according to the rules.[80] He once explained the situation he was aiming for like this: 'You have a model, and you paint a thing to be very close to the model. Then you have the possibility of completely fooling the situation, making one exactly like the other, which doesn't particularly interest me. (In that case, you lose the fact of what you actually have done.) I think what I hoped for was to get very close to that but still to have a sense of what the thing was, what it is. I like that there is the possibility that one might take the one for the other, but I also like that, with just a little examination, it's very clear that one is not the other'.[81] The label looks like the label; something looking like a turpentine and paint spill has run down and across it. The top and bottom rims have been painted with aluminium paint to look like the aluminium of the original can. A high degree of illusion has been achieved by the way it has been painted. It is an illusion enhanced by allowing the object the freedom to occupy without a base any space it is placed in. The possibility is there that you might take it for a Savarin coffee can with seventeen paintbrushes, but when you look at it it becomes clear that it is not a can with brushes in it. *Painted Bronze* does not deceive the eye, and it would not deceive the hand – it is small, but very heavy. Look at it closely and you see that the label has been quite freely painted; the marks signifying individual letters do not become them; and letters refuse to make words. But things are not out of control. Notice the way the turpentine spill has been made to change direction as it partly obscures the first 'a' of 'Savarin' and the 'O' of 'COFFEE', and how each paintbrush handle has been painted and over painted. Look again at the label – see its complex relations of colour and hue. This is complex painting mindful of the medium and playing games with the illusion of shallow space. The finger prints on the brushes make the illusion but the ostentatious orange thumb print on the can, wrinkling the red of the label and pushing the black band of 'COFFEE' into the ground, unmakes it. And not all of the can has been painted over; here and there the bronze of the cast metal and red lead primer breaks the illusion created by the aluminium paint. Also, Johns' touch is everywhere apparent as style and a kind of subjectivity. Each mark is treated as *of* the can, the label, and the brushes and as *of* Johns himself and his identity as an artist concerned with the intimate tactility of pictorial things. In this respect the finger prints and thumb print are tautologies. There are no accidents here, just a lot of highly self-conscious, self-reflexive hand-of-the-artist facticity of the kind associated with modernist painting. It may seem like a sculpture, but, if so, it is a sculpture that has been painted not so much to look like a Savarin coffee can with paintbrushes in it as one which has had painted onto it – so as to be congruent with it – a thoroughly modernist painting of a Savarin coffee can with brushes in it. It is very delicately done but there is no doubt that this is painting stressing the properties of the medium and the flatness of the surface in ways that are supposed to guarantee painting's independence of and resistance to the sculptural. Yet this is modernist painting that has been added to the very three dimensionality that is the province of sculpture. Without a base its three dimensional value as sculpture is depreciated, but it is not negated. *Painted Bronze* (Savarin can and brushes) does not go as far as *Flag* in problematizing the difference between sign and referent, art and life, but it does go further than, for example, *Flashlight I* did in problematizing, in a related way, the difference – and in the discourse of art around 1960 it was for some persons a crucial difference – between painting and sculpture. Not so much a sculpture *about* painting, after all, as a painting *around* sculpture. As its title suggests *Painted Bronze* (Savarin can with brushes) is an object which is neither a painting nor a sculpture but both a painting and a sculpture.

Have you noticed how strange the brushes are? Ferrules and bristles down, soaking in the turpentine. It is not that they should not be like that because that is how Johns kept and presumably still keeps his brushes whilst working. That is part of his and most artists' studio practice. They would, however, have been very difficult to cast with the bristles up. And once cast that way, they would have been more easily and quickly recognised as casts of brushes – hair rarely convinces when cast in bronze – and the uncertainty that *Painted Bronze* was intended to effect would have been greatly diminished. That being the case, there must have been good technical reasons for keeping the brushes bristles down in the can. But they do seem, even in this context, unnecessarily packed together. That's what's strange. Kozloff saw and understood *Painted Bronze* as 'the most epigrammatically paralyzed of all Johns' work… In its isolated presence, it juxtaposes the most lifelike usefulness with the most painful immobility'.[82]

Painted Bronze (ale cans) and *Painted Bronze* (Savarin can with brushes) recur in Johns' art as either indexical or iconic signs. When Johns uses the base of a can to mark or imprint the surface then the trace left behind on the surface has the value of an indexical sign: it is a synecdoche of the whole thing that printed it, and it has a metonymic relation with Johns as the person who did the printing. When he makes a graphic equivalent of the can or uses a photograph of it, recreates or reinterprets the original with a pictorial image resembling it, then the sign has the value of an icon. *Painted Bronze* (ale cans) and *Painted Bronze* (Savarin can with brushes) first appeared as indexical signs in *Field Painting* of 1963–1964 (Collection of the artist) – a Ballantine Ale can and a Savarin coffee can and brushes also appear in this picture attracted by the magnets attached to the three-dimensional letters of the colour names, RED, YELLOW, BLUE, that divide the surface in two. Thereafter, in 1964, *Painted Bronze* (ale cans) was used to provide the image for *Ale Cans*, a lithograph published by Universal Limited Art Editions; and three years later *Painted Bronze (Ale Cans)* and *Painted Bronze* (Savarin can with brushes) were used to provide images for the portfolio *First Etchings* also published by U.L.A.E.

Arrive/Depart of 1963–1964 (Bayerische Staatsgemäldesammlungen, Munich), *Eddingsville* of 1965 (Museum Ludwig, Cologne), *Passage II* of 1966 (Tehran Art Museum, Iran), *Harlem Light* of 1967 (Private collection), *Decoy* of 1971 (Collection of Mrs. Victor Ganz), *Untitled*, 1972 (Museum Ludwig, Cologne), *Corpse and Mirror II* of 1974–1975 (Collection of the artist), *Dutch Wives* of 1975 (Collection of the artist), *Weeping Women* of 1975 (The David Geffen Collection, Los Angeles), *Usuyuki* of 1977–1978 (Collection of the artist), *Between the Clock and the Bed* of 1981 (Collection of the artist), *In the Studio* of 1982 (Collection of the artist) – that is an incomplete listing of the surfaces that carry the indexical traces of a Ballantine Ale can and/or a Savarin coffee can. I take it that in each case the printed circle has a value in excess of that which it has as a reflexive formal device marking and making the surface. The indexical trace comes in place of an object closely associated with Johns – *Painted Bronze* (ale cans) or *Painted Bronze* (Savarin can with brushes) or a Ballantine Ale can or a Savarin Coffee can – and in place of him and his consciousness as author of the surfaces it appears on and in. Having made the Ballantine Ale cans and the Savarin can as sculptures, those cans became his. The can circles are talismanic marks which not only print the surface in quite contingent ways but also have a value to strengthen, sustain, measure and stamp that surface as *of* Johns.

It is interesting to note which of his paintings and sculptures Johns keeps for his own collection. It has been said that the best collection of 'Jasper Johns' is owned by Johns himself.[83] Some pieces, like *White Flag* (Collection of the artist) from the

Castelli show of 1958, were kept because they failed to sell but there cannot have been many items which failed to find buyers after that. He sold *Painted Bronze* (ale cans) but that was partly the point of making it – so that Castelli could sell it. He did make another cast of it for himself in 1964. But *Painted Bronze* (Savarin can with brushes) was never sold or made into an edition or another version. This strikes me as probably significant. My guess – my phantasy – is that it means more to him than *Painted Bronze* (ale cans). Though both sculptures have a use value in his art as repeatable, but not exchangeable, signs, the sculpture that came in place of Johns when something was required to come in place of him was not *Painted Bronze* (ale cans) but *Painted Bronze* (Savarin can with brushes).

A photograph of *Painted Bronze* (Savarin can with brushes) was used on the plain white cover of the catalogue produced for the 1964 retrospective exhibition at the Jewish Museum – what written information there is is all on the back cover. The year before a photograph of *Painted Bronze* (ale cans) against a black background had been used for the front cover of Steinberg's *Metro* monographic essay as published by Wittenborn. It is to the point that whatever value *Painted Bronze* (ale cans) had for illustrating or representing 'Jasper Johns' was quickly displaced onto *Painted Bronze* (Savarin can with brushes). As an iconic sign *Painted Bronze* (Savarin can with brushes) is here anchoring 'Jasper Johns' as author and encouraging the beholder around the exhibition and through the catalogue. The cover brings 'Jasper Johns' and 'Savarin' into a reciprocal relation. 'Savarin' on the can refers us to 'Jasper Johns'. Or, to put that another way, 'Jasper Johns' is here displaced onto 'Savarin'. The name of the philosopher of the kitchen – Jean-Anthelme Brillat-Savarin – as the brand name of a vacuum-packed ready-ground coffee is turned towards the name of the artist whom the catalogue constructs as something of a philosopher of the studio – and a good cook also. The retrospective exhibition gives *Painted Bronze* a context of use on the catalogue's cover but it is a context which is presented as contextless. Isolated, the photograph of *Painted Bronze* effects some of the uncertainty of seeing and telling that the actual *Painted Bronze*, and Johns' work generally, achieves – an uncertainty commented on in the essays in the catalogue. It turns us towards an oeuvre and to 'Jasper Johns' as author of that oeuvre. But thus isolated, that is all it can do.

In 1977 *Painted Bronze* (Savarin can with brushes) provided one of the images used for the cover of the catalogue and the poster (fig. 4) for the retrospective

Fig. 4
Savarin, 1977,
lithograph, edition 8, 48" × 32".
Published by Universal Limited
Art Editions, Inc.,
West Islip, N.Y.

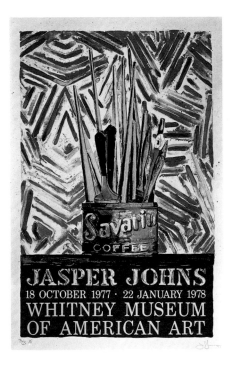

exhibition held at the Whitney Museum of American Art. Two different lithographs were used to make and transfer the images. The one used for the catalogue meant that it appeared on the back cover. The one used for the poster was 'larger than life', but, as Johns said, 'that was a deliberate attempt at advertising' on his part.[84] In each case, for those who know it, the image effects some of the uncertainty with regard to painting and sculpture that *Painted Bronze* effected. But the image is sufficiently different from *Painted Bronze* – the turpentine spill has been cleaned away, the finger print has gone, and the brushes have been made more pristine – to raise the possibility that what is represented here is actually a Savarin coffee can with paintbrushes in it and not the painted bronze coffee can and brushes. The main pictorial signifier on the poster, *Painted Bronze*, or a Savarin can with paint brushes in it, is represented on a wooden surface in front of *Corpse and Mirror II* of 1974–1975. The wood grain becomes the background for information about what is being advertised. There is no mistaking the product for Savarin coffee – though it is important, of course, that the can is a Savarin can and that there are paintbrushes in it. The product is clearly stated in corporate identity stencilled capitals: 'JASPER JOHNS'. The poster has the material significance of a page from an emblem book whose words and images have been brought together and creatively developed into what we now recognise as a personification of 'Jasper Johns'.

As it appears in 1977, in the context of materials associated with the Whitney Museum retrospective, *Painted Bronze* (Savarin can with brushes) returns to classify new work and old work as *of* 'Jasper Johns': painting, sculpture and graphic work. As an iconic sign it recreates something of the undecidability that is so much the point of the original as a 'separate thing' that might be taken for an 'ordinary thing', and as a 'separate thing' that is neither a painting nor a sculpture but both a painting and a sculpture; and to that is added a doubt about whether what the sign *represents* is the original 'separate thing' or merely an 'ordinary thing', a Savarin coffee can with paintbrushes in it, that looks like the original. As the personification of 'Jasper Johns', *Painted Bronze* comes in place at a moment and site of retrospection as a memento associated with a sign of death and reflection. The choice of *Corpse and Mirror II* for the background surface of the poster cannot have been accidental. In this context, *Painted Bronze* has to be understood as a key figure taking part in an extended allegory about reflection and retrospection as the basis of going on where going on can only mean repetition and return or an attempt at restitution, about sexual difference, self-identity, and death – themes that, as we shall see, were secured in Johns' art during 1960–1961.[85]

The New Sculpture   ...*the representative visual art of modernism.*

Clement Greenberg, 'The New Sculpture' (1958), Art and Culture, 1961[86]

In an essay published in 1949 titled 'The New Sculpture', Greenberg glimpsed that modernist painting, in renouncing representation and the illusion of three-dimensionality to the extent that it had in its pursuit of the appeal to eyesight alone, had probably gone as far as it could.[87] It tended, inevitably, towards decoration and 'suffered a certain narrowing of its range of expression'.[88] It tried to compensate for this 'by a greater intensity and concreteness', but that only weakened 'the unity and dynamics' of the picture.[89] 'The fact is,' he wrote, 'that easel painting in the literally two-dimensional mode of our age… may soon be unable to say enough about how we feel to satisfy us quite, and that we shall no longer be able to rely upon painting as largely as we used to do for a visual ordering of experience.'[90] By the time he came to revise 'The New Sculpture', in 1958, for inclusion in *Art and Culture*, the anthologised selection of his critical essays that was published in 1961, he had become convinced that sculpture had begun 'to make itself felt as the most representative, even if not the most fertile, visual art of our time'.[91] Painting continued 'as the leading and most adventurous as well as the most expressive of the visual arts', but sculpture, attending to the problems and character of its means in the pursuit of 'purity', had been able 'to put an ever more higher premium on sheer visibility and an ever lower one on the tactile and its associations' so that, like painting, it could also 'render substance entirely optical'.[92] At the end of the 1950s and the beginning of the 1960s sculpture seemed to offer modernist art a way beyond the narrow range of painting's 'field of possibilities'[93] – but at the cost of turning into painting.

Partisan matters aside, Greenberg was right to firm-up his earlier commitment to the vitality of sculpture. It was around that time, between rewriting 'The New Sculpture' and the publication of *Art and Culture*, that sculpture came to be accorded a priority within modernism that it had not previously received, first in the United States of America, especially in New York, and then in Europe, especially in London. In 1958, David Smith, who had been given a full-scale retrospective at the Museum of Modern Art, New York the year before, was represented at the XXIX Venice Biennale. In the same year John Chamberlain exhibited works made exclusively with crumpled automobile parts, and Carl Andre began making his first large wood sculptures in Frank Stella's studio. In 1959 Donald Judd began writing reviews for *Arts* magazine. And in 1960 Anthony Caro moved his work into abstraction via a trip to Bolton Landing and a close reading of Greenberg's writing. By the end of 1961, Robert Morris had made his 'blank form' sculptures, and Judd was about to realise that his paintings needed more relief and sculptural form. For a while sculpture seemed to be considered not simply as an interesting form of modern art to be made and thought alongside painting but as the practice with which to expose and explore the very condition of artistic modernism. Greenberg, according to the logic of his own understanding of the development of painting, and no doubt attentive to the art-talk of the day, had, in 1958, picked up on a shift in theory and practice.

Johns must have begun making sculptures at more or less the same time that Greenberg began rewriting 'The New Sculpture' and what he made and Greenberg wrote were partly determined by the implications of what had been achieved in Abstract Expressionism. For both Johns and Greenberg, the new sculpture derived its impetus from the concerns of modernist painting and took form as a kind of three-dimensional painting. But in different ways. Johns' sculpture was made from a rejection or denial of Abstract Expressionism; the sculpture that Greenberg came to value aspired to emulate it. At the end of 'The New Sculpture', Greenberg affirmed the work he had in mind in Rilkean terms: it was its 'physical independence, above all,' that contributed to 'the new sculpture's status as the representative visual art of modernism'; it did not have 'to carry more than its own weight', nor did it have 'to be *on* anything else, like a picture'; it existed 'for and by itself literally and conceptually'; it had a 'self-sufficiency... wherein every conceivable as well as perceptible element' belonged 'altogether to the work of art'.[94] More than anything, it was this belief in self-sufficiency, which Greenberg regarded as 'the positivist aspect of the modernist "aesthetic" ' most fully realised in sculpture,[95] that Johns' sculpture problematised so effectively.

Having made *Painted Bronze* (ale cans) and *Painted Bronze* (Savarin can with brushes), Johns does not seem to have been interested in making more sculptures that articulated and disarticulated the difference between painting and sculpture, 'separate thing' and 'ordinary thing', and so on. Sculpture became a major concern for him only at the moment when the integrity of sculpture became a matter central to the problems of modernity in art. He took some of the undecidability of *Flag* into sculpture and effected some of its hermeneutic intrigue there. And having done that, he seems to have decided that he had no reason to make more of that kind of sculpture. (**Light Bulb** was produced in 1962 as a way of using an imperfect cast that had been made in 1960. Painting the cast covered the imperfection. The printed label, 'General Electric, 100 Watt, 120 V', and logo, works well as a flat sign on the surface, but there was no way that the interior of the 'bulb' – the exhaust tube, fuse, stem press, lead-in wires, support wires and filament – could have been represented so as to achieve the same degree of illusionism that had been achieved on the surface of *Painted Bronze* (ale cans) and *Painted Bronze*.) We should not forget that Johns took *Flag* as his beginning in art. Painting was his major concern. Not sculpture. Johns would return to *Flag* and continue making the Stars and Stripes in its like. It was an object that, situated at the edge between art and life, could not be transcended, only repeated, but it was worthwhile repeating it. It seems not to have been worthwhile repeating *Painted Bronze* (ale cans) and *Painted Bronze* (Savarin can with brushes), or not as sculptures. Johns continued making sculpture after 1960, but the sculptures were made as asides to his preoccupation with painting. This does not mean, however, that works such as **High School Days** of 1964 and **Subway** of 1965 should not be taken seriously.[96] Some things need only to be said, or can only be said effectively, as asides. Once said, some of these asides might have to be seen and understood as possessing an importance over and above what they are as 'separate things', especially with regard to their significance in relation to the central concerns of a body of work or to the work as a whole. It seems to me that this is how we should see and understand **Memory Piece (Frank O'Hara)** of 1961–1970 and *Untitled*, 1987.

Memory Piece

identifying
To lose the possibility of recognizing
2 similar objects —
    2 colors, 2 laces
hats, 2 forms whatsoever
to reach the Impossibility of
    visual
    sufficient memory
to transfer
from one
    like object to another
the memory imprint
————Same possibility
with sounds; with brain facts

Marcel Duchamp, *The Green Box, The Bride Stripped Bare by Her Bachelors, Even*[97]

Seeing a thing can sometimes trigger the mind to make another thing. In some instances the new work may include, as a sort of subject matter, references to the thing that was seen. And, because works of painting tend to share many aspects, working itself may initiate memories of other works. Naming or painting these ghosts sometimes seems a way to stop their nagging.

Jasper Johns to Richard Francis, 1982[98]

I have forgotten my loves, and chiefly that one,…

Frank O'Hara, 'In Memory of My Feelings'[99]

A knife, fork, spoon and a deep plate were cast in wax. The knife, fork and spoon were then placed within the plate's rim and positioned on its base so they supported each other at an angle. The blade of the knife is wedged between two of the fork's four tines and the spoon rests against a third. A minimum amount of wax was used to bond the knife and spoon to the fork and each item to the plate. The whole thing was then cast in bronze to function as the superstructure of a fountain made for the courtyard of the New York house that Johns moved into in 1987.[100] Installed and working, the bronze structure rests on a feed pipe and pump mechanism above a rectangular trough of water. The pipe directs a jet of water through a hole in the centre of the plate. The jet rises to make contact with the cutlery just above the handle of each item, falls onto the plate, and then overflows into the trough. Although the structure is physically above the water, it seems to float on it in a fixed position: an effect caused by the fact that it vibrates slightly as it responds, balanced on the feed pipe, to the movement of the pump and the water's spurt and fall. This is Johns' most recent sculpture to date: *Untitled*, 1987 (fig. 5).

Johns' practice is knowingly reflexive: retrospective and self-examining. He often visits past works, as he did when he made the poster for the 1977 Whitney Museum exhibition, and uses bits of them in new works, fragments that are fragmented in their turn. It must be difficult for him to know, when he makes these visits, whether he has moved forward or degenerated. It's probably neither and both.

Reflection, like memory, is an instance of the reconsideration or recollection of something that, but for its action, might be lost or forgotten. If forgetting was not such a selective process we should not remember anything. Absolute forgetting is inconceivable, and the onerous weight of what is remembered can have a paralysing effect on thought and action unless it is dealt with.[101] Johns' work bears witness to this relation between memory and reflection. It evidences an attempt to keep past works and past moments present, to reconsider them, work on and with them. The persistence of memory and reflection is basic to Johns' practice, and was established even before he became interested, in 1959, in Duchamp's *Green Box* note about memory and things: 'to reach the Impossibility of sufficient visual memory to transfer from one like object to another the memory imprint'.[102] Indeed, it was

Fig. 5
Untitled, 1987, bronze (fountain), 9" × 10¹/₈" diameter.
Collection of the artist.

established at his beginning as an artist when he 'dreamed one night of painting a large flag' and afterwards began to paint one. *Flag* came out of a dream, and then existed in a relation of association with a childhood memory of parental separation, loss, and naming.[103] It was made at the moment when Johns decided to be an artist and destroyed all the work he had made prior to it. 'Jasper Johns', the artist, began in a moment of self-retrospection and self-destruction that would reverberate throughout his art as a continual self-reckoning. I think that this is how we should see and understand *Untitled*, 1987; as one more instance of self-reckoning, one in

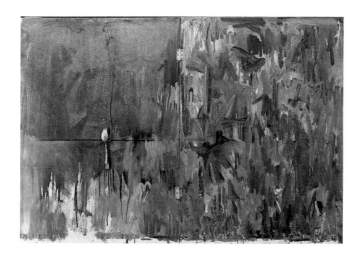

Fig. 6
In Memory of My Feelings –
Frank O'Hara, 1961,
oil on canvas with objects
(2 panels), 40" × 60".
Collection of
Stefan T. Edlis, Chicago.

which were consolidated things and memories that had concerned Johns for over thirty years.

Johns began using cutlery in his art in 1961. That was when he bound together a spoon and a fork with a straightened wire coat-hanger, the convex surface of the bowl against the concave surface of the tines, and suspended them from the top of one of two canvases hinged together to make a single picture with an immovable surface (fig. 6). The spoon and fork have swung from side to side and have scratched an arc in the paint. The picture's title *In Memory of My Feelings – Frank O'Hara* has been stencilled across the lower edge of both canvases. 'In Memory of My Feelings' has been taken from the title of a poem that O'Hara wrote in 1956; it was published in 1958, and anthologised in 1960.[104] 'Frank O'Hara' names the author of 'In Memory of My Feelings' and turns the picture towards him as its dedicatee. *In Memory of My Feelings – Frank O'Hara* is both *of* O'Hara's poem and *of* O'Hara. 'J. Johns '61' is also stencilled there, authenticating the picture as *of* Johns.

O'Hara, Associate Curator of Painting and Sculpture at the Museum of Modern Art, was a figure of frenetic centrality in the artistic culture of New York in the 1950s and 1960s.[105] The literature of that culture constructs him with fondness and affection as a poet and playwright, a critic, friend and collaborator with artists. Between 1955 and 1965 he lived with Joe LeSeur with whom he had a complex relationship. Most people assumed they were lovers, but they were not.[106] For some of the time that Johns knew him, O'Hara was in love with Vincent Warren, a dancer with the Metropolitan Opera, the Henry Street Playhouse, Living Theatre and Judson Church.[107] A cycle of fifty poems, written by O'Hara between 1959–1961, records the progress of his relationship with Warren: *Love Poems (Tentative Title)*. O'Hara also loved, and was loved by several women, one of whom, the painter Grace Hartigan, is the dedicatee of the poem 'In Memory of My Feelings'.

Johns and O'Hara seem to have got to know each other around 1957.[108] By the summer of 1959 they were friends, and remained so until the poet's death in 1966. O'Hara's interest in Johns was in his work.[109] And both shared a passion for poetry. In July 1959 O'Hara wrote to Johns about Jack Kerouac's *Doctor Sax*, recommended that he read the work of Gary Snyder, Philip Whalen, and Mike McLure, and compared Robert Duncan and Charles Olson as West Coast and East Coast poets.[110] References to Johns also turn up in O'Hara's poetry at about this time. In August, in 'Joe's Jacket', O'Hara and Johns, with Vincent Warren, entrain to Southampton, Long Island, for a weekend party at Janice and Kenneth Koch's house – this was where O'Hara fell in love with Warren.[111] The next year in 'What Appears To Be Yours' O'Hara is 'zooming downtown' to Johns.[112] Friendship turned into something of a working relation. In 1963 they began collaborating on a portfolio of prints and poems.[113] And before that, in 1961, Johns had begun making an object whose title, *Memory Piece (Frank O'Hara)*, situates it in a relation of association with O'Hara's poem 'In Memory of My Feelings' and his own painting *In Memory of My Feelings – Frank O'Hara*.

Memory Piece (Frank O'Hara) starts as a drawing of an object. Along the drawing's lower edge Johns has stencilled, in almost the same way that they are put in place on *In Memory of My Feelings – Frank O'Hara*, the object's title, his name, and the date: 'Memory Piece (Frank O'Hara) J. Johns '61'.[114] The drawing, which Johns gave to O'Hara, was made in the manner of diagram to illustrate some specifications for the benefit of a fabricator. Here are the instructions for making a wooden chest with three drawers and a hinged lid on top: each drawer is to be lined, base and sides, with lead, and then filled with sand; each drawer front is to be fitted with a ring pull so that the drawer can be slid in and out; the underside of the lid is to be fitted with the cast of a foot that should be set in place, all around it, with lead or sculp-metal; the metallic or metal-like surface is to be titled and authored with raised letters as per the stencilled information provided. In 1961 work on *Memory*

Piece (Frank O'Hara) progressed no further than the drawing and taking a rubber cast of the sole of one of O'Hara's feet – the first body fragment cast since 1955. The object was eventually completed in 1970 with the cast set in sculp-metal to the depth of the lid. The sculp-metal has been rubber stamped with the legend (above the toes) 'MEMORY PIECE (FRANK O'HARA)', and (below the heel) 'Jasper Johns 1961–1970'. When the lid closes it prints the sand – South Carolina sand from Edisto Beach – with O'Hara's foot.

On April 10, 1963, O'Hara sent Johns a letter poem, 'Dear Jap', in which he mentions the drawing – 'I miss my drawing which I think you are still looking at' – and the cast made for *Memory Piece (Frank O'Hara):*

> I want someday
> to have a fire-escape
>
> in 1951 I became crazy for fire-escapes
> as you remember
>
> when I think of you in South Carolina I think of my foot in the sand
>
> do you at some strange distance
> think of glass boxes full of weeds[115]

The mention of the work-in-progress on *Memory Piece (Frank O'Hara)* is obvious, but the reference to memory, and the way it makes the meaning of what comes before and after it multivalent, is easily missed. A lot depends on 'as you remember'. What does Johns remember? That in 1951 O'Hara became crazy for fire-escapes? Had O'Hara told Johns about the trip he had made to Chicago with Jane Freilicher in the summer of 1951? They had stayed overnight at the YMCA, where Freilicher read Norman Mailer's *The Naked and the Dead* and heard a man make a suicide leap from a floor above hers.[116] Or did he expect Johns to have picked up the reference in 'In Memory of My Feelings'?

> Five years ago, enamoured of fire escapes, I went to Chicago,
> an eventful trip; the fountains! the Art Institute, the Y
> for both sexes, absent Christianity.
> At 7, before Jane
> was up, the copper lake stirred against the sides
> of a Norwegian freighter[117]

And when Johns 'at some strange distance think[s]', is that 'strange distance' a spatial or temporal remove? It is probably both. When it is temporal, the reference is to memory. What 'glass boxes full of weeds' does Johns remember? When it is spatial, the reference is to the geographical distance between O'Hara, in New York, and Johns, in South Carolina. 'As you remember when I think of you in South Carolina… my foot in the sand.' Here Johns is supposed to remember, or is imagined remembering, while the poet thinks of the artist and remembers having his foot cast two years before. And what about the 'fire-escapes'? It seems that every reference in the poem is meant to be taken several ways, so it is probably more than a reference to the Chicago trip. (O'Hara himself lists three possible meanings for John Bernard Myers' recipe for a hard-boiled stuffed-egg!) If 'fire-escape' is, as seems likely, heavily troped, it might be turned towards a desire to own or rent a place away from the restrictions of Manhattan at or near the beach on Fire Island; or it might refer to a way of getting free of the control or danger of a person, or even free of a 'self', for there is a very emphatic 'I' repeated throughout the poem. Does O'Hara connect the steps of 'a fire-escape' with Johns' *Memory Piece (Frank O'Hara)*? It seems that he does.

In 1961, as Johns once pointed out, the 'mood changes' in the progress of his art.[118] His subject matter and mode of representation changed. It was as if he became a different type of artist. The paintings are predominantly grey in their colour range and titled in such ways as to connote emotional conditions: of being deceived – *Liar* (Collection of Tony Ganz); of denial and negation – *No* (Collection of the artist); of coldness – *Water Freezes* (Private collection); of anguish or a desperate Ugolino-like hunger – *Painting Bitten by a Man* (Collection of the artist); and of feelings and persons remembered – *In Memory of My Feelings – Frank O'Hara*.

In Memory of My Feelings – Frank O'Hara, which was painted some five years before the poet's death, cannot be explained as an in memoriam for O'Hara. But using the title of the poem and the name of its author to make and title the surface may have enabled Johns to produce a painting which seemed to represent his own feelings, something he had not been able to do or had not wanted to do, perhaps, since *Target with Plaster Casts*. Here the words 'In Memory of My Feelings – Frank O'Hara' function as a kind of hinge between the painting and O'Hara's poem, designating difference and articulation, marking a correspondence and cooperation between the meanings which proliferate for the painting and the poem, the painter and the poet, their practices and lives. Attending to *In Memory of My Feelings – Frank O'Hara* in this way produces a surface that represents Johns' feelings, and something of the story of his life, by way of a contiguous relation with the meanings of the poem and the life story of the poet.

'In Memory of My Feelings' has been valued not only as the best of O'Hara's autobiographical poems but also as 'one of the great poems of our time'.[119] It is a poem whose central themes are memory and self – 'a self that threatens continually to dissipate under the assault of outside forces'.[120] Grace Hartigan read it as defining ' "inner containment" – "how to be *open* but not violated, how *not to panic*" '.[121] It is not a poem in which the poet recalls events; it is not about what has happened. For most of the poem what the poet recalls is how he felt, or how he feels about how he felt, when something happened. 'New feelings generate new selves', and 'from the midst of the poet's many selves a vision of an essential self emerges – a self that is always *becoming* but never is content to be singly what it is, a self that constantly asserts "I am *not* what I am," and is determined to escape beyond the boundaries of a fixed personality.'[122] The image of the serpent, the poem's leitmotif, has been taken to represent either 'the poet's true self – the self that must triumph if he is to become an artist' or 'the essential self that must be preserved despite the constant passing away of one identity after another'.[123] The serpent's turn comes at the end of the poem after a clear statement of the impossibility of forgetting:

> And yet
> I have forgotten my loves, and chiefly that one, the cancerous
> statue which my body could no longer contain,
>
> against my will
> against my love
>
> become art,
> I could not change it into history
> and so remember it,
> and I have lost what is always and everywhere
> present, the scene of my selves, the occasion of these ruses,
> which I myself and singly must now kill
> and save the serpent in their midst.[124]

These last lines give us a love that could not be forgotten and that against the poet's will and love has 'become art', and a 'scene of selves' that has been lost but remains everywhere present. What are we to make of this? In a sense we do not have to make anything of it because whatever we do make of it will not necessarily access what Johns made of it in 1961. And what Johns made of it is realised in and as the surface of *In Memory of My Feelings – Frank O'Hara*.

In Memory of My Feelings – Frank O'Hara does not illustrate O'Hara's poem. The painting refers to the poem, and by referring to it alludes obliquely to its main themes of feelings remembered and scenes of selves. Though the painting, to borrow some words from the poem's first line, 'has a man in it' he is hardly 'transparent'. I take it that the 'feelings' are there on the surface of the two canvases and that the 'man in it' is underneath. The grey brushstrokes that dominate the right canvas and mark the white ground and thinned brown-greyness of the left canvas are there not as the direct expression of feelings but as signifiers of the expression of feelings appropriated from the pictorial language of Abstract Expressionism. In the context of Johns' surfaces they refer to the idea of the unmediated association of feelings and facture, but their very identity as appropri-ated signifiers inhibits our seeing and understanding them as marks directly expressive of Johns' feelings. Beyond that, the appropriated expressive gestures make a willed surface that negates loves and selves while, at the same time, putting a self in place. By the early 1960s brushstrokes like these had become an integral component of Johns' repertoire of surface mechanisms. As they enter *In Memory of My Feelings – Frank O'Hara* they mark it, albeit at a certain remove, as *of* Johns. They function as a signature brush-marking which guarantees authorship, keeps past present and comforts us that the strangely novel is never completely new. But they also obscure and hide other surface matter laid down in primary and secondary colours. They almost bury the words 'DEAD MAN' which are stencilled across the lower edge of both canvases: 'D' on the left canvas, 'EAD MA[N]' on the right, and then, over that, but only on the right canvas, again – this time in smaller letters – 'DEAD MAN'. And they completely cover the human skull that Johns pictured – probably with a crude stencil of his own devising – in the top right of the right canvas. You can make it out from its pentimenti.[125]

Portrait – Viola Farber (Private collection), begun in 1961 and finished in 1962, has been seen as 'a direct variation on' *In Memory of My Feelings – Frank O'Hara*.[126]

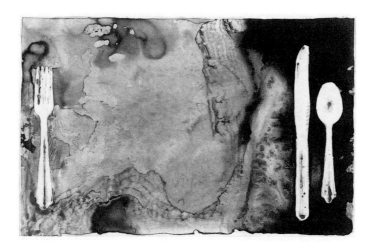

Fig. 7
Study for 'In Memory of My Feelings', 1967, ink and graphite pencil on plastic, 12¹/₄" × 19". Collection of the artist.

Perhaps it is. It is larger, but not that much larger; it is painted mostly in greys; it uses a hinged canvas; and its 'VIOLA' has been stencilled with superimposed capitals in more or less the same place in the same manner as 'DEAD MAN'. Here the spoon and fork get their next context of use after *In Memory of My Feelings – Frank O'Hara*, each bent to make a right angle, fixed to the surface as if to function as brackets, and joined by a rubber band. The hinged canvas above them can be unhooked and pulled down to reveal its back side painted grey, the open space into which it had been inserted, and, through the opening, the wall behind it. If some of these mechanisms come into this surface from or via *In Memory of My Feelings – Frank O'Hara* where in a relation of association does 'VIOLA' come from? Viola Farber, who had been a featured dancer in the Merce Cunningham Company since the mid 1950s, was, like O'Hara, one of Johns' friends. Perhaps the use of her name on the surface and in the title hinges something about her and her dancing to Johns' painting in much the same way that O'Hara and 'In Memory of My Feelings' had been hinged to *In Memory of My Feelings – Frank O'Hara* with its spoon and fork. Or perhaps 'Viola' works, as 'Frank O'Hara' did, by contiguous association with another.

But why the fork and spoon, bound together and suspended from the top of *In Memory of My Feelings – Frank O'Hara*? Are they connected by some family resemblance to the other household objects – the Ballantine Ale can, the Savarin coffee can, light bulb and flashlight, and so on – which find themselves in Johns' studio and thence in his art? Or do they signify in some more distinctive sense? I should make it clear that to ask such questions is not to invite a reply which organises Johns' practice into a rational iconography. The point is rather that coherence might be found in the underlying mechanisms of reference and association, mechanisms that might explain the coherence of the appearance of the cutlery in the fountain *Untitled*, 1987.

In 1967 Johns illustrated O'Hara's 'In Memory of My Feelings' for a posthumous edition of a selection of his poetry published by the Museum of Modern Art, New York (fig. 7).[127] The principal illustration is of a place setting: a knife, fork and spoon. At the end of the poem there is a single spoon. One of O'Hara's poems – a poem associated by him with 'In Memory of My Feelings' – was titled 'Dig my Grave with a Silver Spoon'.[128] It seems likely that there is some private set of associative references or meanings at work in *In Memory of My Feelings – Frank O'Hara* between Johns and O'Hara, Johns and O'Hara's poem, the poem and death (metaphorical and actual – for the Chicago suicide can be read between some of the lines), the poem and feelings felt when something happened, a love that could not be forgotten and which became art, a self and a scene of selves that was lost and is everywhere present, and a spoon and fork – and a knife; a set of moves or 'games' in a language which signifies to those who know the language and its terms and are able to perceive its significance. We realise this because the mechanisms of language are public. We know the language but not the dictionary. To say that cutlery signifies death, etc., is not to say that it signifies death, etc., wherever it appears. The meaning of the cutlery depends on the context of its use in each specific work.[129] However, the genesis of an image, especially one that signifies by contiguous association with another image or object, goes to some kind of consistency, just as the genesis of an image may be what serves to determine appropriate contexts of use.

Memories. The impossibility of forgetting. Loves. Selves. Feelings. Death. Naming. We can now begin to reconstruct some of the contiguities and relations of human experience which Johns may associate with the cutlery in the paintings made in 1961. The years 1954–1961 were the years in which Johns and Robert Rauschenberg were together as a couple. Sometime in 1961 they began to move apart, and by the time the summer of 1962 ended, they were no longer together. Evidently, according to gossip, 'the break was bitter and excruciatingly painful, not

Fig. 8
Voice, 1964–1967, oil on canvas with objects
(2 panels), 96¼" × 69¼".
The Menil Collection, Houston.

only for them but for their closest associates – Cage and Cunningham, and a few others – who felt that they, too, had lost something of great value'.[130] There are two more bits of gossip which seem relevant to understanding the change in Johns' work in 1961 and the significance of *In Memory of My Feelings – Frank O'Hara*. Johns may have known that in 1960, the year prior to making *In Memory of My Feelings – Frank O'Hara*, O'Hara's relationship with Grace Hartigan had ended. Evidently between 1951 and 1960 Hartigan and O'Hara 'saw each other or spoke on the phone almost every day. They frequently spent weeks – even months – together in the country… In 1960, after a major quarrel with Frank, Grace left New York, married, and settled in Baltimore. She sent him a strongly worded letter breaking off all relations. They did not see each other again for five years, and then only briefly'.[131] O'Hara's 'In Memory of My Feelings' written in 1956 may have been read somewhat differently in 1961. The intimacy between the poet and the poem's dedicatee by then terminated, the poem would have gained a new context for reading and a changed biographical reference which maybe Johns utilises. Perhaps – this is my second bit of gossip – it is also significant for the analysis of the possible references mobilised in *In Memory of My Feelings – Frank O'Hara* that Johns, who was there when it began in July 1959, would have known in the summer of 1961 that O'Hara's love affair with Warren was ending. The last of O'Hara's *Love Poems*, 'A Chardin in Need of Cleaning', is dated July 6, 1961.

Spoons, forks, and knives are, like the Ballantine Ale can and the Savarin coffee can, persistent objects, iconic and indexical signs, in Johns' art. For example, to give just some of their sitings: *Out of the Window Number II* of 1962 (Collection of the artist) has a spoon attached to it; *Passage* (Museum Ludwig, Cologne), also of 1962, has a fork, as does *According to What* of 1964 (Private collection); another fork turns up in *Eddingsville* of 1965; and *Diver* of 1964 (Irma and Norman Braman Collection) has a fork, spoon and knife. In 1967, Johns attached a spoon and fork suspended, but not tied together, by a wire at the side of *Voice* (fig. 8), a painting that he had begun in 1964. At least one commentator on his art has implied that this was done in memory of O'Hara who had died in 1966.[132] In 1979 and 1980, spoons, forks and knives and casts of spoons, forks and knives were incorporated into the frames of two pictures, both titled *Dancers on a Plane*. Discussion of the *Dancers on a Plane* paintings will return us to *Untitled*, 1987.

Dancers on a Plane, 1979, (fig. 9) has a fascinating crosshatch patterned surface that interpellates a puzzled and puzzling beholder. We are expected to think about what kind of surface it is, and what kind of painting we are looking at. We are supposed to work it out, and to see a solution in its mirrored vertical halves and its horizontally divided sub-sections. And we are supposed to take delight in its ritualistic, even obsessive, technical complexity. The stencilled words along the lower edge contribute to the effect:

ENRCJEORHSNOSN1A9P7L9AJNAESDPAF..

Fragmented and made disjunctive they make evident the materiality of writing. So we attend to them as surface matter, as a pattern of elements. Of course, we puzzle them out and make them read 'DANCERS ON A PLANE, JASPER JOHNS, 1979', and quite likely we realise that they indicate a cylindrical possibility for the surface. In other words, they are arranged like that not only to name and authorise the surface but also to generate their bit of it in ways compatible with the rest of it. But what is the meaning of the crosshatched surface in its relation of

Fig. 9
Dancers on a Plane, 1979, oil on canvas
with objects, 77⁷/₈" × 64".
Collection of the artist.

association with the idea of dancers on a plane and with whatever is signified by the cutlery painted white and fixed to the verticals of the white frame? This is a different kind of puzzle. Given what we know about Johns' art, surely we are not expected to understand the crosshatching as a metaphor for the kinds of movements that dancers make. Though it would be possible to see it as a reference to that moment early in the twentieth century when painters were interested in the idea of representing movement and the kinds of representations that they made of it. Francis Picabia's *danseuse étoile* or *édtaonisl* pictures of 1913, *Edtaonisl (ecclesiastic)* (The Art Institute, Chicago) and *Catch-as-catch-can* (Philadelphia Museum of Art), come to mind as precedents, but not necessarily as resources, for Johns' pictures. That possibility should be sufficient to make us sceptical about the idea that the hatching pattern is a metaphor of dancing or dancers. However, this is not to say that the surface is not turned towards some dancers or one dancer in particular; this is a 'mirrored' surface and the plural might refer to a single dancer

Fig. 10
Nepal, 17th century,
*The Terrible Devata Samvara, who has
seventy-four arms, with his female wisdom
(sakti) with twelve arms*, gouache on cloth,
28" × 19". Ex-collection Ajit Mookerjee;
present location unknown.

and his or her reflection. Nor is *Dancers on a Plane* about cutlery where cutlery is
understood to be a metaphor for 'consuming' painting or dance. What is happening
on and as the surface mediates that kind of purely projective assumption. We have
to start thinking with a degree of historical specificity about the kinds of contiguity
that might exist between what is there and the ideas that we are generating about it.
Connotation is at the edge. And we know, because we have glimpsed some of the
meanings which might be associated with cutlery as it has been used in Johns' art,
that what is connoted by it is unlikely to be peripheral. 'The plane's edge
beckons.'[133]

Dancers, sex and death. Sometime in 1979, Johns became interested in a
seventeenth-century Nepalese painting of the Devata Samvara simultaneously
dancing and copulating with his female wisdom (sakti) (fig. 10) that was illustrated
in Ajit Mookerjee's book *Tantra Art*.[134] He was especially struck by the Samvara's
necklace of skulls and by way the artist had represented the act of sexual

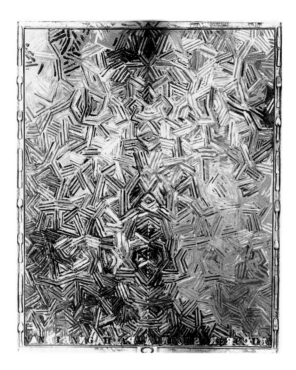

Fig. 11
Dancers on a Plane, 1980,
oil on canvas with painted bronze
frame and objects, 78³/₄" × 63³/₄".
The Tate Gallery, London.

penetration. Johns had wanted to incorporate the testicles and penis from the Tantra painting as part of *Dancers on a Plane*, but had not been able to do so successfully.[135] Maybe that failure helps explain the presence of the cutlery. In the Tantra painting signifiers of sexual penetration are placed in a relation of association with signifiers of death, and the references to death in *In Memory of My Feelings – Frank O'Hara*, signified in a relation of association with cutlery. In this chain of contiguity, the cutlery at the edge of *Dancers on a Plane* has to be understood as a displaced signifier of other more conventional signifiers of sex and death. Johns was interviewed in 1989 and questioned about the cutlery in *Dancers on a Plane* and the works that related to O'Hara. He replied, 'My associations, if you want them, are cutting, measuring, mixing, blending, consuming – creation and destruction moderated by ritualized manners'.[136] The move that Johns makes in giving these associations seems immense. He begins with precise, intimate physical actions and ends with highly abstract notions. Cutting, measuring, mixing, blending, consuming are easily understood as actions associated with preparing and eating food and with producing and consuming art. It is not so easy to grasp how cutlery might be associated with making the violence and extremeness of originating and ending something more acceptable as social behaviour or as a way of life. Except, perhaps, by contiguous association. Given what we know about Johns' characteristic protocols and procedures when it comes to making art, it is possible to glimpse the way he might be using cutlery to refer to sex and death and 'creation and destruction' in ways that make the reference less painful, violent or extreme, if only for himself. The signifiers are mundane, as are the first associations, but the chain ends with the grand metaphysical themes of creation and destruction. These are the themes signified by the union of Samvara and his sakti. They are, in a sense, the Tantra painting's ideal: the 'creative process and absolute cessation' as a single principle wherein there is neither affirmation nor denial, neither purity nor impurity, neither form nor formlessness but a bringing together of all these dualities.[137] And it is this ideal that Johns appropriates to the crosshatched pattern and its associated thematics which becomes *Dancers on a Plane*. The appropriation is, however, to an ideal already established in Johns' art which makes the moderating use of cutlery appropriate at the plane's edge. Interviewed about the painting in 1991 or early 1992, Johns said that he was looking at Tantric art, 'thinking about issues like life and death, whether I could even survive. I was in a very gloomy mood at the time I did the picture, and I tried to make it in a stoic or heroic mood. The picture is almost uninflected in its symmetry. There is no real freedom. The picture had to be executed in a very strict fashion or it would have lost its meaning'.[138] This particular scene of self could only be handled ritualistically.

Dancers on a Plane, 1980, (fig. 11) uses the same crosshatched pattern but changes coloration. It is a much darker painting – 'the ominous sequel' as one commentator put it.[139] Here Johns replaced his own name with that of Merce Cunningham, breaking it and interspersing its letters with the now mirrored or reversed letters of the title:

NANDIƎNИGAHⱵAꟼMAMИEORƧCЯEƎCƆUИ .

The trope directs us not only to the possibility of a cylindrical surface but also to one which seems as if it could be read from the back as well as the front – a trope set by *Flag*. More to the point for my analysis are the signifiers of sexual penetration that Johns has managed to incorporate in the bronze frame along with the knives, forks and spoons now also cast in bronze. The scrotum is there at the bottom below the central 'A'; the penile shaft is above it, across the surface, in the triangle at the centre of the top framing edge. These signifiers have been taken from the Nepalese painting of the Samvara. The vertical line which divides the Samvara's scrotum into its blue and green halves is there in Johns' picture scraped through the grey paint, as are the hairs growing out of it. The skulls are represented by the row of white dots which, equal to half the width of the canvas, travel almost half way across the centre of the surface; this has been taken from the white dots of Samvara's necklace of skulls.[140]

Dancers. Creation and destruction. Life and death. An 'I' that needed to survive. Cutlery. You could take *Dancers on a Plane* as another version of *In Memory of My Feelings – Frank O'Hara*, its main themes dealt with this time not by reference to O'Hara but to Merce Cunningham, another close friend, a choreographer and dancer, and, a name no doubt turned, as was 'Frank O'Hara' in 1961, towards another person and another scene of self. Whatever the historically specific references are that might be associated with *Dancers on a Plane* they exist in a contiguous relation of association with the themes associated with *In Memory of My Feelings – Frank O'Hara*.

> *I don't see them.*
> *There. The dancers are there, invisible – an analogue to racing thoughts.*
> *Framed by the utensils of eating.*
> *A meal to be eaten?*
> *An invisible meal.*
> *Two meals: one light, one dark. One sprightly, one stained with sexual dread.*
> *Dancers on a plate?*
> *No. They need more space than that.*
>
> Susan Sontag, 'In Memory of their Feelings'[141]

We need to fill in the gaps between the cutlery associated with and used to illustrate 'In Memory of My Feelings' (fig. 7) and between the knives, forks and spoons at the edges of *Dancers on a Plane* (figs. 9 & 11). And this we can do with

Fig. 12
Souvenir, 1964, encaustic on canvas with
objects, 28³/₄" × 21". Collection of the artist.

reference to two paintings that Johns made during a visit to Japan in 1964: *Souvenir* (fig. 12) and *Souvenir 2* (Collection of Mrs Victor Ganz). These are painted surfaces with things attached. Common to both is a working flashlight positioned to throw its beam onto a rear-view mirror that has been angled as if to reflect onto a ceramic plate printed with the words RED, YELLOW and BLUE and a passport-type photograph of Johns. *Souvenir*: a memory token; a thoroughly self-reflexive work; and the only recognisable self-portrait of the artist to date. Johns may have associated the *Souvenir* paintings with Duchamp's *Green Box* note on 'the memory imprint'.[142] He was 'Thinking anything could be a souvenir of something else, not specifically a self-portrait. Ego was not clear. Maybe just another way of dishing up a Johns'.[143] The 'ego', often mistaken for the 'self', is geographically, dynamically and economically, never clear in its defence of the personality as a whole. And, 'maybe'.

It took *Souvenir*'s 'not specifically a self-portrait' memento twenty-three years to receive its next context of use in Johns' art. Knife, fork, spoon and plate come together as *Untitled*, 1987 (fig. 5). On one level, *Untitled*, 1987, is, of course, 'just another way of dishing up a Johns', an excellent fountain, but an aside to Johns' main concerns. On another level, it is a 'complete' and 'separate thing' of central importance that has to be seen and understood as a complex allegory of sex, life and death; of dancing and dancers; of the constant replacement of one self-identity by another; and of the impossibility of forgetting memories, feelings, loves, 'and chiefly that one,… become art'.

Sketchbook Notes

Have made a silk-screen of Baudelaire's description of sculpture as an inferior art. Use this in VOICE *(2) or somewhere else. Perhaps fragment it so that its legibility is interfered with.*

Jasper Johns, 'Sketchbook Notes', *Juilliard*, 1968–69[144]

I thought that that painting [Voice 2] *would break down into many different kinds of focus that would provide you with different kinds of information, and that there would be no real organising principle. I had hoped that the painting could be distributed in space and shown backwards and forwards, upside down. But it didn't work out.*

Jasper Johns, 1995[145]

The ale cans and the brushes in the coffee can, those were an idea for sculpture, and I saw them as things which existed in air and that could be moved around. That one could move around them… Something like that enters in the sculptures because they are thought to be things that could be seen from a constantly changing point of view.

Jasper Johns, 1995[146]

The note 'have made a silk-screen' could refer to a silk-screen which has been made or to the intention to have a silk-screen made. In 1968 Johns had at least one silk-screen made that was used to transfer an image of a text to work-in-progress on a painting.[147] However, he does not recall having made a silk-screen of 'Baudelaire's description of sculpture as an inferior art'. Nor does he recall what he read about Baudelaire's views on sculpture.[148] Nevertheless, it seems likely, when he made his note, that he would have had in mind that section of *The Salon of 1846* wherein the French critic outlines his views on 'Why Sculpture Is Tiresome'.[149] Baudelaire thought that painting had several advantages over sculpture. As far as he is concerned, in *The Salon of 1846*, a painting can only be looked at on its own terms; it has a single surface and a unique point of view; it is only what it means to be and there is no other way of looking at it. A sculpture, on the other hand, is looked at on the beholder's terms: it exhibits too many surfaces at once, and the beholder is free to choose what to look at, and from whatever point of view; it is vague and ambiguous, and it is also affected by chance tricks of light. Johns' views on painting and sculpture, as they pertain to his own work, were contrary to those of Baudelaire. What Baudelaire saw as the advantages of painting, Johns would have seen as disadvantages; and what Baudelaire saw as the disadvantages of sculpture, Johns would have seen as the advantages.

It is perhaps not without interest that Baudelaire's views on sculpture could have easily cropped up in 1967 or 1968 in more or less any conversation about Michael Fried's essay 'Art and Objecthood'. Fried's essay was published in *Artforum* in June 1967 and anthologised in Gregory Battcock's *Minimal Art: A Critical Anthology* in 1968.[150] As presented in 'Art and Objecthood', Fried's views on minimal art, or, as he preferred to call it, 'literalist' art, art that he identified as of a corrupted sensibility, were close to Baudelaire's on sculpture. And his views on the art he valued, modernist art, a painting by Kenneth Noland or Jules Olitski, or a sculpture by Smith or Caro, were close to Baudelaire's on painting. Minimal art was vague and ambiguous, and too much *of* the beholder and the beholder's field of vision. Modernist art, no matter where it was encountered, was exclusive of the beholder, whom it affected as a 'wholly manifest' work with a distinct and unambiguous, instantaneous 'entire presentness'.[151]

Voice 2 (fig. 13) – the painting the note suggests might be a suitable place to use a silk-screen of 'Baudelaire's description of sculpture as an inferior art' – can be seen, in this context, as a thoroughly anti-Baudelairean painting. It is made of three canvasses that butt together to represent a curved space. Each canvas can be moved about, horizontally and vertically, to make at least three different configurations of the overall surface. This is how Johns described what he was trying to do:

> …I hoped that the three panels in *Voice 2* might be able to accommodate any order or disorder; might be upside down, sideways, backwards. While working in this way, trying to make the painting have no 'should be', trying to make it any way it wanted to be, the 'should be' seemed amusing; but working with that idea became too difficult for me, too complicated. I couldn't deal with it and settled for the more simple order.[152]

Fig. 13
Voice 2, 1968–1971, oil and collage on canvas (3 panels), 72" × 162".
Öffentliche Kunstsammlung Basel, Kunstmuseum.

But what of the silk-screen image that was used for *Voice 2*? That is a photograph of the hanging spoon and fork that had been attached to *Voice* (fig. 8) in memory of Frank O'Hara. Let us assume that this image can be associated with the silk-screen mentioned in the sketch book note. How might it be seen as representing 'Baudelaire's description of sculpture as an inferior art'? The image began while Johns was making a lithograph version of *Voice*. He made a photograph of the wire with the spoon and fork to have a litho-plate made of it, and indicated on the photograph that the 'fork should be 7" ', so that when the plate was made the objects could be printed to their actual size. The people who made the litho-plate included the written instruction with the image. The instruction was removed when Johns made the lithograph of *Voice*, but, before that, the unaltered plate was photographed and a silk-screen was made of it. The silk-screen, considerably enlarged, was used for several works in 1968, including the various *Screen Piece* (fig. 14) paintings.[153] As it is glimpsed in *Voice 2*, the fork should be 7".

Fig. 14
Screen Piece 3 (The Sonnets),
1968, oil on canvas,
72" × 50". Private collection.

It is difficult to know in what ways Johns may have thought the photo-image of the hanging spoon and fork, where the 'fork should be 7"', illustrated 'Baudelaire's description of sculpture as an inferior art'. If he did. But it could have had something to do with its 'should be'. For Baudelaire the 'should be' of painting was taken as secure, while sculpture could be anything the beholder wanted it to be or it contingently came to be according to how it was exhibited. I guess Johns thought the image illustrated something of that contingency. As such, it was a good image with which to try to make a painting that had no 'should be' and that could be seen in any way that the exhibitor or beholder thought it 'should be' seen.

The Critic Sees   *I had the idea that in society the approval of the critic was a kind of cleansing police action. When the critic smiles it's a lopsided smile with hidden meanings. And of course a smile involves baring the teeth. The critic is keeping a certain order, which is why it is like a police function.*

Jasper Johns to Michael Crichton, 1977[154]

I was hanging a show of sculpture and drawings, and a critic came in and started asking me what things were. He paid no attention to what I said. He said what do you call these? and I said sculpture. He said why do you call them sculpture when they're just casts? I said they weren't casts, that some of them had been made from scratch, and others had been casts that were broken and reworked. He said yes, they're casts, not sculpture. It went on like that.

Jasper Johns to Michael Crichton, 1977[155]

Between 1959 and 1966, Johns made three sculptures that commented on experiences with critics and their lack – or carelessness – of perceptivity: *The Critic Smiles*[156]; *The Critic Sees* (fig. 15); and *Summer Critic* (Private collection). The best of these sculptures, *The Critic Sees*, was produced in response to a three-minute visit of a critic to one of his exhibitions – probably the exhibition of sculptures and drawings at the Castelli Gallery, January–February, 1961.[157] A second version of *The Critic Sees* was made in 1964. For the purposes of this essay, despite their differences, the two sculptures, *The Critic Sees* and **The Critic Sees II**, can be referred to as if they were one.

The Critic Sees is a brick of plaster, anthropomorphised, and with an emphatic axis of focus, that interpellates the beholder in a very direct way. On its facade is a cast of spectacles, behind the lenses of which are set casts of Johns' mouth, one with the teeth together, the other with the teeth apart;[158] and everything covered with layers of smoothed and burnished sculp-metal. *The Critic Sees* makes a joke about art critics and art criticism: the critic is blind, he sees with his mouth. However, getting the joke does not exhaust the sculpture's meaning and value for it comments on much more than the blind verbosity of art critics.

Of all those persons who have attended to Johns' art, only Kozloff has paid extended attention to *The Critic Sees*. What he wrote about it at the beginning of his 1969 monograph on Johns is especially interesting. Kozloff gets the joke, and then moves beyond it to point out that:

the piece is figuratively endowed with a sensory capacity of its own. Not only does it have an inner and outer structure, but it also carries the suggestion that human senses – insofar as they are referred to by facial fragments – are contained by the work, which thereby confronts the spectator in an almost animate guise. Or, rather, it should be said that faculties, rather than the senses, indicate the point at issue. For verbal activity, or possibly that from which it derives, conceptual thinking, is juxtaposed to the process of vision. …Taken in itself the object would imply, not that sight is more important than speaking, but that they are peers, brought together in an unnatural situation (with the further discrimination that the speech element might be seen as active or passive).

Overall, then, *The Critic Sees* is a presentation of two activities concerned not only with works of art, of course, but with the human reception of the visual world: sight and verbal articulation. Within their context here it is impossible to tell whether speech has usurped vision, or vision has capped speech. The probability remains that they are necessarily mutual reinforcements, components of an integrated function. But it is just as reasonable to suppose that they are displacements rather than extensions of each other, with all that that suggests of resistance and disorientation. That either interpretation is possible is merely one attribute of the muteness of visual art – which can be literal and tangible, but not explicit, in its meaning. Johns accentuates this muteness in an effort to underline the spectator's dilemma. If his 'statement' is open-ended and unresolved, so too, he seems to be saying, is our relation to art. His is a reverie on the potentialities of and the obstruction to what can be learned. Without at least an initial intimation of this uncertainty, and the pressure it exerts, no viewer fully experiences a work of art which sidetracks all categories. (Is *The Critic Sees*, for instance, a life cast, a still life, an object, or a sculpture – and if a sculpture, is it a bas-relief?) For one moment in his career the artist externalises, perhaps even allegorizes, the dialogue in which 'the prime motive of any work is the wish to give to discussion, if only between the mind and itself'.[159]

In other words, *The Critics Sees* is a personification of something in which seeing and speaking, as powers of the mind, are brought together in such a way that neither is privileged, yet both are essential, and each has, by displacement or extension, taken the place of the other. *The Critic Sees* effects disorientation and resistance in

Fig. 15
The Critic Sees, 1961, sculp-metal over plaster with glass, 3¹/₄" × 6¹/₄" × 2¹/₈". Private collection.

the beholder that is as much an aspect of our relation to the visual world as it is of our relation to art. If the beholder, looking at *The Critic Sees*, does not have an inkling that this is so, he or she will not be able to understand what he or she is looking at, or, by extension, any thing. In bringing together signs of seeing and speaking in this way, Johns produced an allegory not only of the effect of allegory but also of theory.

Current usage has it that 'theory' is a supposition or system of ideas explaining something, especially one based on general principles independent of the particular things to be explained; a bit of abstract knowledge or speculative thought; or the exposition of the principles of a practice – theory as distinct from practice. There is, however, something lacking in current usage – and that is the beholder or observer.

This definition of theory, taken from *The Shorter Oxford English Dictionary*, includes the observer: 'A scheme or system of ideas or statements held as an explanation or account of a group of facts or phenomena; a hypothesis that has been confirmed or established by observation or experiment, and is propounded or accepted as accounting for known facts; a statement of what are held to be the general laws, principles, or causes of something known or observed'. 'Theory' comes from the Greek verb 'theorein', to look at, to contemplate, to survey, from 'theoros' spectator, and from 'theoria' a group of spectators. But this is not only looking and the spectators are not any spectators. In Greece the 'theoria' were individuals of probity and status in the polity who were summoned to attest to the occurrence of some event, to witness it and to verbally certify that it had taken place. Their function was to see-and-tell. Other persons could see-and-tell but only that which the 'theoria' saw-and-told had any social standing. Only the theoretically attested to could be treated as fact. The 'theoria' saw, and how it told what it had seen effected an object of knowledge. Theories don't just find their objects, they constitute them, which is to say that the individual agents, working collectively, do the constituting. Theory is certainly not independent of theory, of what it has previously constituted as knowledge, nor is it interest free. One cannot stand outside language and context and see and tell what is being looked at from a point of purely disinterested reason. The idea of theory as inclusive of phenomena and reference is valuable precisely because it holds that the phenomenal – the material object – is the basis of perception, consciousness, cognition, the logic of understanding, and that understanding is constructed in and by language. It moves our understanding away from theory as speculative knowledge to an emphasis on theory as a determining, mediating, interfering and reciprocating relation between seeing   and seeing material objects, events, and so on – and the representation in speech and/or writing of what has been seen. The object becomes an object of knowledge only when and because it becomes an effect *of* theory, and there is only theory because *of* the object that the 'theoria' come together to see and certify.[160] It is here that the so-called 'resistance to theory' can be located: in the materiality of the object looked at (which if it is a manufactured thing will include its willed figuration); and in the way the object has been seen and told which is 'a resistance to language itself or to the possibility that language contains factors or functions that cannot be reduced to intuition'.[161] Theory is always in need of more theory.

The Critic Sees not only provides a commentary on the problem of theorising sculptures and paintings and things, 'separate things' and 'ordinary things', but it also interrogates any beholder who tries to theorise it. The interrogation began with *Flag*, an object that invites the beholder – Johns being its first beholder – to testify to it, and simultaneously interrogates him or her about how she is seeing and telling it. Johns' art is allegorical. He has, as Kozloff pointed out, developed a practice based on the supposition that ' "things" have no intrinsic value', that there is no equivalence between a thing and what it represents.[162] A work by Johns must be understood not as having a meaning but as presenting or in the case of *The Critic Sees* confronting the beholder with several meanings. The beholder has to constitute meaning. But meaning can never be fixed. Theory doesn't work like that. In front of any thing, trying to make sense of it, we are always making and unmaking the meaning of what we see, and of our selves. This is the knowledge that is effected by the best of Johns' 'separate things'. That's what the critic sees.

Since what we think is never what we see.

Wallace Stevens, 'What We See Is What We Think', *The Auroras of Autumn*[163]

— *Say it, no ideas but in things* —

William Carlos Williams, 'Book One', *Paterson*[164]

I tend to focus upon a relationship between oneself and a thing that is flexible, that can be one thing at one time and something else at another time. I find it interesting, although it may not be very reassuring.

Jasper Johns to Christian Geelhaar, 1979[165]

Flag, 1960
Sculp-metal and collage on canvas
13" × 19³/₄"
Lent by Robert Rauschenberg

Flag, 1960
Plaster
$12^{7}/_{8}"$ × $19^{3}/_{8}"$ × $1^{1}/_{16}"$
Collection of the artist

Flag, 1960
Bronze, edition # 4/4
$12^{1}/_{8}" \times 18^{5}/_{8}" \times {}^{1}/_{4}"$
Collection of the artist

Flag, 1960
Plaster and painted wood frame
12$^{9}/_{16}$" × 19$^{1}/_{8}$" × 1$^{1}/_{16}$"
Collection of the artist

Flag, 1960
Resin
$13^{1}/_{6}"\times19^{5}/_{8}"\times1^{5}/_{8}"$
Collection of the artist

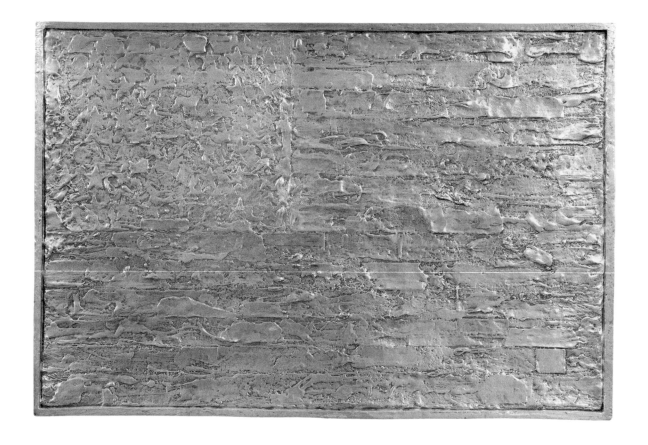

Flag, 1960
Silver
12³/₄" × 19¹/₄" × 1¹/₂"
Collection of the artist

Light Bulb I, 1958
Sculp-metal,
4¹/₂" × 6³/₄" × 4¹/₂".
Private collection

[Shown in Houston only]

Light Bulb II, 1958
Sculp-metal
5" × 8" × 4"
Collection of the artist, on loan
to the Philadelphia Museum of Art

Light Bulb, 1960
Plaster
4$^{1}/_{8}$" × 5$^{7}/_{8}$" × 4"
Collection of the artist

Light Bulb, 1960
Bronze, edition # 2/4
4^{1}/$_{4}$" × 6" × 4"
Courtesy Leo Castelli

Light Bulb, 1960
Painted bronze, edition # 4/4
4¹/₄" × 6" × 4"
Collection of the artist, on loan
to the Philadelphia Museum of Art

Untitled, 1960–61
Plaster and wire
3¹/₄" × 12" × 6¹/₂"
Collection of the artist

Bronze, 1960–61
Bronze, edition # 2/2
3^{1}/$_{4}$" × 11^{1}/$_{2}$" × 6^{1}/$_{4}$"
Collection of the artist

English Light Bulb, 1970
Sculp-metal
4³/₄" × 3¹/₈" × 4¹/₄" – 6" (height variable)
Collection of Mark Lancaster

Flashlight I, 1958
Sculp-metal over flashlight and wood
$5^{1/4}$" × $9^{1/8}$" × $3^{7/8}$"
Sonnabend Collection

Flashlight II, 1958
Papier mâché and glass
4" × 8³/₄" × 3"
Lent by Robert Rauschenberg

Flashlight III, 1958
Plaster and glass
5 1/4" × 8 1/4" × 3 3/4"
Collection of the artist

Flashlight III, 1958
Bronze, glass and aluminium paint
5^1/$_8$" × 8^1/$_8$" × 3^3/$_4$"
Private collection, New York

Flashlight, 1960
Bronze and glass, edition # 2/3
$4^7/8$" × 8" × $4^1/2$"
Collection of the artist, on loan
to the Philadelphia Museum of Art

Ale Cans, 1960
Plaster
$5^3/_4$" × $8^1/_8$" × $4^3/_4$"
Collection of the artist

Painted Bronze, 1960
Painted bronze, edition # 2/2
5$^1/_2$" × 8" × 4$^1/_2$"
Collection of the artist, on loan
to the Philadelphia Museum of Art

Painted Bronze, 1960
Painted bronze
13$^{1}/_{2}$" × 8" diameter
Collection of the artist,
on loan to the
Philadelphia Museum of Art

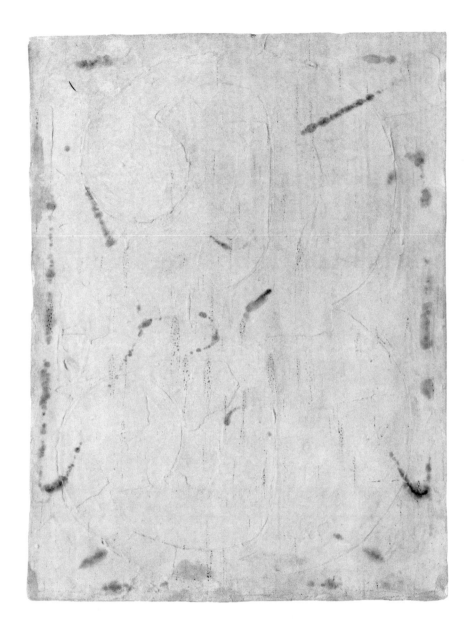

Figure 3, 1961
Plaster and wire
$26^{1}/_{4}$" × 20" × $1^{5}/_{8}$"
Collection of the artist

0 through 9, 1961
Plaster
27" × 20^1/$_2$" × 2^1/$_2$"
Collection of the artist

0 through 9, 1961
Aluminium, edition # 1/4
26" × 19⁷/₈" × 1¹/₄"
Collection of the artist

Numbers, 1963–78
Aluminium relief
57⁵/₈" × 43⁵/₈" × 1³/₈"
Collection of the artist

High School Days, 1964
Sculp-metal over plaster with mirror
4¹/₄" × 12" × 4¹/₂"
Collection of the artist, on loan
to the Philadelphia Museum of Art

Subway, 1965
Sculp-metal over plaster and wood
7⁵/₈" × 9⁷/₈" × 3"
Collection of the artist, on loan
to the Philadelphia Museum of Art

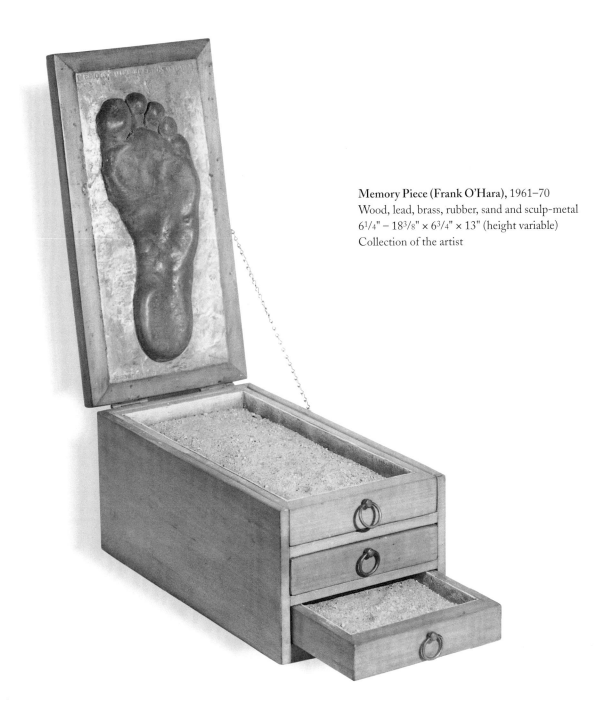

Memory Piece (Frank O'Hara), 1961–70
Wood, lead, brass, rubber, sand and sculp-metal
6¼" – 18³/₈" × 6¾" × 13" (height variable)
Collection of the artist

The Critic Smiles, 1959
Sculp-metal
1⁵/₈" × 7¹/₄" × 1¹/₂"
Collection of the artist, on loan
to the Philadelphia Museum of Art

The Critic Sees II, 1964
Sculp-metal over plaster with glass
3¹/₄" × 6¹/₄" × 2¹/₈"
Collection of the artist, on loan
to the Philadelphia Museum of Art

CHECKLIST OF EXHIBITS

Flag, 1960
Sculp-metal and collage on canvas
13" × 19³/₄"
Lent by Robert Rauschenberg

Flag, 1960
Plaster
12⁷/₈" × 19³/₈" × 1¹/₁₆"
Collection of the artist

Flag, 1960
Bronze, edition # 4/4
12¹/₈" × 18⁵/₈" × 1/₄"
Collection of the artist

Flag, 1960
Plaster and painted wood frame
12⁹/₁₆" × 19¹/₈" × 1¹/₁₆"
Collection of the artist

Flag, 1960
Resin
13¹/₆" × 19⁵/₈" × 1⁵/₈"
Collection of the artist

Flag, 1960
Silver
12³/₄" × 19¹/₄" × 1¹/₂"
Collection of the artist

Light Bulb I, 1958
Sculp-metal,
4¹/₂" × 6³/₄" × 4¹/₂".
Private collection
[Shown in Houston only]

Light Bulb II, 1958
Sculp-metal
5" × 8" × 4"
Collection of the artist, on loan
to the Philadelphia Museum of Art

Light Bulb, 1960
Plaster
4¹/₈" × 5⁷/₈" × 4"
Collection of the artist

Light Bulb, 1960
Bronze, edition # 2/4
4¹/₄" × 6" × 4"
Courtesy Leo Castelli

Light Bulb, 1960
Painted bronze, edition # 4/4
4¹/₄" × 6" × 4"
Collection of the artist, on loan
to the Philadelphia Museum of Art

Untitled, 1960–61
Plaster and wire
3¹/₄" × 12" × 6¹/₂"
Collection of the artist

Bronze, 1960–61
Bronze, edition # 2/2
3¹/₄" × 11¹/₂" × 6¹/₄"
Collection of the artist

English Light Bulb, 1970
Sculp-metal
4³/₄" × 3¹/₈" × 4¹/₄" – 6" (height variable)
Collection of Mark Lancaster

Flashlight I, 1958
Sculp-metal over flashlight and wood
5¹/₄" × 9¹/₈" × 3⁷/₈"
Sonnabend Collection

Flashlight II, 1958
Papier mâché and glass
4" × 8³/₄" × 3"
Lent by Robert Rauschenberg

Flashlight III, 1958
Plaster and glass
5$^{1}/_{4}$" × 8$^{1}/_{4}$" × 3$^{3}/_{4}$"
Collection of the artist

Flashlight III, 1958
Bronze, glass and aluminium paint
5$^{1}/_{8}$" × 8$^{1}/_{8}$" × 3$^{3}/_{4}$"
Private collection, New York

Flashlight, 1960
Bronze and glass, edition # 2/3
4$^{7}/_{8}$" × 8" × 4$^{1}/_{2}$"
Collection of the artist, on loan
to the Philadelphia Museum of Art

Ale Cans, 1960
Plaster
5$^{3}/_{4}$" × 8$^{1}/_{8}$" × 4$^{3}/_{4}$"
Collection of the artist

Painted Bronze, 1960
Painted bronze, edition # 2/2
5$^{1}/_{2}$" × 8" × 4$^{1}/_{2}$"
Collection of the artist, on loan
to the Philadelphia Museum of Art

Painted Bronze, 1960
Painted bronze
13$^{1}/_{2}$" × 8" diameter
Collection of the artist,
on loan to the
Philadelphia Museum of Art

Figure 3, 1961
Plaster and wire
26$^{1}/_{4}$" × 20" × 1$^{5}/_{8}$"
Collection of the artist

0 through 9, 1961
Plaster
27" × 20$^{1}/_{2}$" × 2$^{1}/_{2}$"
Collection of the artist

0 through 9, 1961
Aluminium, edition # 1/4
26" × 19$^{7}/_{8}$" × 1$^{1}/_{4}$"
Collection of the artist

Numbers, 1963–78
Aluminium relief
57$^{5}/_{8}$" × 43$^{5}/_{8}$" × 1$^{3}/_{8}$"
Collection of the artist

High School Days, 1964
Sculp-metal over plaster with mirror
4$^{1}/_{4}$" × 12" × 4$^{1}/_{2}$"
Collection of the artist, on loan
to the Philadelphia Museum of Art

Subway, 1965
Sculp-metal over plaster and wood
7$^{5}/_{8}$" × 9$^{7}/_{8}$" × 3"
Collection of the artist, on loan
to the Philadelphia Museum of Art

Memory Piece (Frank O'Hara), 1961–70
Wood, lead, brass, rubber, sand and
sculp-metal
6$^{1}/_{4}$" – 18$^{3}/_{8}$" × 6$^{3}/_{4}$" × 13" (height
variable)
Collection of the artist

The Critic Smiles, 1959
Sculp-metal
1$^{5}/_{8}$" × 7$^{1}/_{4}$" × 1$^{1}/_{2}$"
Collection of the artist, on loan
to the Philadelphia Museum of Art

The Critic Sees II, 1964
Sculp-metal over plaster with glass
3$^{1}/_{4}$" × 6$^{1}/_{4}$" × 2$^{1}/_{8}$"
Collection of the artist, on loan
to the Philadelphia Museum of Art

BIOGRAPHY

1930	Jasper Johns, born 15 May 1930, in Augusta, Georgia.
1940–48	Attends the University of South Carolina, Columbia, for three semesters.
1949–51	Enrols in commercial art school in New York City but leaves after two semesters. Works as a messenger boy and shipping clerk until drafted into the U.S. Army. Stationed at Fort Jackson, South Carolina. For last six months of service stationed at Sendai, Japan.
1952–54	Returns to New York. Works as a clerk in a bookstore. Introduced to Robert Rauschenberg and begins to help him make objects to be used in window displays. Meets John Cage and Merce Cunningham. Gives up his job in the bookstore, decides that he is an artist, and begins to make *Flag*.
1955	Completes *Flag*, *Target with Plaster Casts*. By the end of the year he has also made *White Flag*, *Flag Above White*, *Flag Above White with Collage*, *Target with Four Faces*, and the number paintings *Figure 1*, *Figure 2*, *Figure 5* and *Figure 7*.
1957	*Green Target* is exhibited in 'Artists of the New York School, Second Generation' at the Jewish Museum. *Flag* is exhibited in 'New Work' at the Castelli Gallery. Leo Castelli becomes Johns' dealer.
1958	Castelli holds the first exhibition of Johns' works in January–February. The Museum of Modern Art, New York, acquires *Target with Four Faces*, *Green Target* and *White Numbers*. Makes first sculptures, *Light Bulb I*, *Light Bulb II*, *Flashlight I*, *Flashlight II* and *Flashlight III*.
1959	Nine paintings included in 'Sixteen Americans' at The Museum of Modern Art, New York.
1960	Makes *Painted Bronze* (ale cans) and *Painted Bronze* (Savarin can with brushes).
1961	Buys house at Edisto Beach, South Carolina. Paints *Liar*, *In Memory of My Feelings – Frank O'Hara*, *No*, *Painting Bitten by a Man*.
1962–63	Moves into an apartment on Riverside Drive. Works there and in South Carolina. Becomes founding Director of the Foundation for Contemporary Performance Arts, Inc. George Wittenborn publishes *Jasper Johns* by Leo Steinberg, the first monograph on the artist.
1964	Retrospective exhibition at the Jewish Museum, New York, travels to the Whitechapel Gallery, London. Visits Japan where he paints *Watchman*, *Souvenir* and *Souvenir 2*. Returning to New York, he paints *According to What*.
1965	Retrospective exhibition at the Pasadena Art Museum, Pasadena, CA.

1966	Fire destroys his Edisto Beach house and studio.
1967	Becomes Artistic Adviser to the Merce Cunningham Dance Company. Moves from Riverside Drive to the Provident Loan Society building on Houston Street. Introduces the flagstone motif in *Harlem Light* and paints *Screen Piece*.
1969	Max Kozloff's *Jasper Johns* is published.
1970	Acquires home and studio on St. Martin, French West Indies.
1972	Paints the large *Untitled* (Museum Ludwig) on four panels, incorporating cast body parts and his first use of the crosshatch motif.
1973	Moves to Stony Point, New York.
1974	The Arts Council of Great Britain organises 'Jasper Johns Drawings', with catalogue 'Interview' by David Sylvester, shown at Oxford, Sheffield, Coventry, Liverpool, Leeds and London.
1977	'Jasper Johns' retrospective at the Whitney Museum of American Art, travels to Cologne, Paris, London (Hayward Gallery), Tokyo and San Francisco.
1978	Executes decor for Merce Cunningham's 'Exchange', his last work as Artistic Adviser for the Company.
1984	Richard Francis' *Jasper Johns* is added to the Abbeville Modern Masters Series.
1986	'Jasper Johns: A Print Retrospective' opens at The Museum of Modern Art, New York.
1987	Moves into house on East Sixty-Third Street, New York, and makes *Untitled*, 1987, for the courtyard.
1988	'Jasper Johns: Work Since 1974' chosen for the American Pavilion at the XLIII Venice Biennale, where Johns is awarded the Grand Prize, the Golden Lion.
1989	'Dancers on a Plane. Cage. Cunningham. Johns', shown at Tate Gallery Liverpool and the Anthony d'Offay Gallery, London.
1990	'The Drawings of Jasper Johns', a comprehensive retrospective of drawings, opens at The National Gallery of Art, Washington, and travels to the Kunstmuseum Basel and the Hayward Gallery, London.
1993	*Jasper Johns. 35 Years. Leo Castelli* published to celebrate Castelli's long relationship with Johns.

REFERENCES

1   I am indebted to Penelope Curtis and Adrian Rifkin for reading a first draft of this essay, and to Alex Potts for the critical attention he gave a later draft (and for his conversation about sculpture and 'things' around Nine Standards Rigg and afterwards). I am grateful to Sarah Taggart for her assistance, and for the sculp-metal. Finally, my thanks go to Jasper Johns for his kindness, and for taking time-out to talk about the work.

2   Joseph E. Young, 'Jasper Johns: An Appraisal', *Art International* (September 1969), p. 54.

3   John Cage, 'Jasper Johns: Stories and Ideas', *Jasper Johns*, exh. cat.; The Jewish Museum, New York (1964), p. 22; Whitechapel Gallery, London (1964), p. 28–29.

4   Michael Crichton, *Jasper Johns* (New York, 1977), p. 26: 'One day in 1954, Jasper Johns, then twenty-four, methodically destroyed all the work in his possession. This was the first of several acts of self-destruction by an artist who would eventually be known for his skill and daring in rebuilding his past.' See also Johns quoted by Mark Stevens and Cathleen McGuigan, 'Super Artist: Jasper Johns, Today's Master', *Newsweek* (24 October 1977), p. 42: 'It was an attempt to destroy some idea about myself... It gets to sound very religious, which I don't like, but it's true.'

5   Rachel Rosenthal, in conversation with the author, 9 June 1992, recalled that *Cross* 'was built of wood, and then had collage. The wood... was like a frame; and the frame was... thick and the collage was at the bottom, and the wood came up from that; and then that was covered with glass; and it was an object. And I loved it so much that I said to him "You do me a star." That was the origin of *Star.*'

6   Leo Steinberg, 'Jasper Johns', *Metro*, 4/5 (1962); revised and published as *Jasper Johns*, (New York, 1963); further revised and reprinted as 'Jasper Johns: The First Seven Years of His Art' in *Other Criteria: Confrontations with Twentieth-Century Art* (New York and Oxford, 1972), pp. 17–57. See 'Jasper Johns: The First Seven Years of His Art', *Other Criteria*, p. 35 and p. 36.

7   Roberta Bernstein, *Jasper Johns' Paintings and Sculptures 1954–1974. 'The Changing Focus of the Eye'* (Ann Arbor, Michigan, 1985), p. 219 n. 53.

8   Johns quoted by Michael Crichton, *Jasper Johns*, p. 30. See also Alan R. Solomon, 'Jasper Johns', *Jasper Johns*, exh. cat., The Jewish Museum, New York (1964), p. 9; Whitechapel Gallery, London (1964), p. 11.

9   W. J. T. Mitchell, '*Ut Pictura Theoria*: Abstract Painting and Language', *Picture Theory* (Chicago and London, 1994), p. 238.

10   James Ayres, *The Artist's Craft. A History of Tools, Techniques and Materials* (Oxford, 1985), p. 161.

11   Jasper Johns in conversation with the author, 22 September 1995.

12   For a discussion of how Johns' art evidences a marked preference for compositions based not on metaphor but on other tropes which either use a part to refer to the whole (synecdoche) or turn the meaning of one thing towards that of another thing with which it is closely, but probably only incidentally associated (metonymy), see Fred Orton, 'Present, the Scene of... Selves, the Occasion of... Ruses' in *Foirades/Fizzles: Echo and Allusion in the Art of Jasper Johns*, exh. cat. ed. James Cuno, The Grunwald Center for the Graphic Arts, Wight Art Gallery, University of California, Los Angeles (1987) and Fred Orton, *Figuring Jasper Johns* (Boston: Harvard University Press and London: Reaktion Books, 1994). For the argument that Johns' work is strategically structured as allegory, always signifying otherwise, challenging our usual habits of seeing and understanding, and effecting doubts in any discourse that tries to explain and value it, see Fred Orton, Chp. 3 'Figuring Jasper Johns' in *Figuring Jasper Johns*.

13   *United States Statutes at Large*, LXI, Chp. 389, 1947, p. 642.

14   Alan R. Solomon, 'Jasper Johns', *Jasper Johns* (New York, 1964), p.8; (London, 1964), p. 9.

15   'Interview' by David Sylvester in *Jasper Johns Drawings*, exh. cat.; The Arts Council of Great Britain (London, 1974), p.13.

16   Emile de Antonio and Maurice Tuchman, *Painters Painting* (New York, 1984), based on transcripts from the film *Painters Painting* made by Emile de Antonio in 1972, p. 97.

17   Leo Steinberg, 'Jasper Johns: The First Seven Years of His Art', *Other Criteria*, p. 25.

18   Alan R. Solomon, 'Jasper Johns', *Jasper Johns* (New York, 1964), p. 8; (London, 1964), p. 9.

19   'Interview' by David Sylvester in *Jasper Johns Drawings*, p. 13.

20   I have developed this way of explaining *Flag's* effect from reading Jacques Derrida's writing on signs that have an undecidable value. For some examples of 'undecidables' see Jacques Derrida, *Positions*, trans. and annotated by Alan

Bass (London, 1987), pp. 42–43. For further discussion of all the issues raised here see Fred Orton, *Figuring Jasper Johns*, Chp. 2 'A Different Kind of Beginning', pp. 89–146.

21   Johns quoted in Leo Steinberg, 'Jasper Johns: The First Seven Years of His Art', *Other Criteria*, p. 31: 'Using the design of the American flag took care of a great deal for me because I didn't have to design it…. So I went on to similar things like targets… things the mind already knows. That gave me room to work on other levels.'

22   Robert Rosenblum, 'Jasper Johns', *Arts* (January 1958), p. 52.

23   Ibid.

24   Ben Heller, 'Jasper Johns' in B. H. Friedman, ed., *School of New York: Some Younger Artists* (New York and London, 1959), p. 35.

25   Andrew Bush, 'The Expanding Eye: The Allegory of Forgetting in Johns and Beckett' in *Foirades/Fizzles: Echo and Allusion in the Art of Jasper Johns* (1987), p. 132.

26   Ben Heller, 'Jasper Johns', *School of New York: Some Younger Artists*, p.35.

27   Leo Steinberg, 'Jasper Johns: The First Seven Years of His Art', *Other Criteria*, p. 37.

28   See the photograph in *Jasper Johns. 35 Years. Leo Castelli*, exh. cat. ed. Susan Brundage, Leo Castelli Gallery, New York (1993), n.p.

29   Rainer Maria Rilke, *Auguste Rodin*, trans. Jesse Lamont and Hans Trausil (New York, 1945) quoted from Albert Elsen, ed., *Auguste Rodin: Readings on His Life and Work*, (Englewood Cliffs, New Jersey, 1965), p. 115.

30   'Interview' by David Sylvester, *Jasper Johns Drawings*, p. 8.

31   Stuart Preston, 'Real and Surreal in the Week's Exhibitions, Dada Revisited', *New York Times*, 25 October 1959, II, p. 23.

32   Leo Steinberg, 'Jasper Johns: The First Seven Years of His Art', *Other Criteria*, p. 37. See also Guillaume Apollinaire, *The Cubist Painters*, trans. Lionel Abel (New York, 1962), p. 22, for the passage Steinberg had in mind: 'The object, real or illusory, is doubtless called upon to play a more and more important role. The object is the inner frame of the picture, and marks the limits of its profundity, just as the actual frame marks its external limits.'

33   Ibid.

34   Alan R. Solomon, 'Jasper Johns', *Jasper Johns* (New York, 1964), p. 10; (London, 1964), p. 13.

35   Max Kozloff, *Jasper Johns* (New York: Meridian Books, 1974), p. 17.

36   Jasper Johns in conversation with the author, 22 September 1995.

37   This drawing, *Light Bulb*, 1957, is illustrated in Nan Rosenthal, Ruth E. Fine and Amy Mizrahi Zorn, *The Drawings of Jasper Johns*, exh. cat.; National Gallery of Art, Washington, D.C. (1990), p. 141.

38   Roberta Bernstein, *Jasper Johns' Paintings and Sculptures 1954–1974*, p. 51.

39   Jasper Johns in conversation with the author, 22 September 1995.

40   Roberta Bernstein, *Jasper Johns' Paintings and Sculptures 1954–1974*, p. 51.

41   Note the drawing *Light Bulb*, 1958, illustrated as fig. 5, in Nan Rosenthal's 'Drawing as Rereading', Nan Rosenthal, Ruth E. Fine and Amy Mizrahi Zorn, *The Drawings of Jasper Johns*, p.23.

42   Note the drawing *Sketch for Flashlight*, 1958, illustrated as fig. 30c in Nan Rosenthal, Ruth E. Fine and Amy Mizrahi Zorn, *The Drawings of Jasper Johns*, p. 148.

43   William Tucker, *The Language of Sculpture* (London, 1974), p.99.

44   Roberta Bernstein, *Jasper Johns' Paintings and Sculptures 1954–1974*, p. 52. Roni Feinstein, 'New Thoughts for Jasper Johns' Sculpture', *Arts* 57 (April 1980), pp. 139–145 has claimed that the light bulb and flashlight sculptures are 'erotic objects' that have 'sexual connotations' and 'serve as metaphorical surrogates for the male genitals'. She sees *Light Bulb II* as 'naked, impotent, its tortured wire evoking a certain angst' and *Flashlight I* as 'held erect and charged with a certain potency'. She also regards Johns' sculpture of 1958–1961 'as an expression of his admiration for the art, intellect, and person of Marcel Duchamp'. She claims that the 'art and thought' of Duchamp were 'the source of inspiration' of the light bulb and flashlight sculptures. I remain unconvinced by Feinstein's claims regarding the eroticism and sexual connotations of Johns' sculptures – especially of the verticality of *Flashlight I* – and the idea that Duchamp was in any way a resource for them. Johns did not become interested in Duchamp's work until after the Castelli show, January–February 1958. That was when he read *The Dada Painters and Poets* edited by Robert Motherwell, and went with Robert Rauschenberg to see the Arensberg Collection at the Philadelphia Museum of Art. I guess that *Comb*, 1916, *A Bruit Secret (With Hidden Noise)*, 1916, *Air de Paris (50cc of Paris Air)*, 1919, and *Why Not Sneeze Rose Sélavy?*, 1921, might have been on show, but it is difficult to see how they could have served as resources for Johns' sculptures of light bulbs and flashlights, assuming that they had not been made at the time of the visit. Duchamp's *Female Fig Leaf*, 1950, *Objet-Dard*, 1951, and *Wedge of Chastity*, 1954, the 'erotic objects', did not gain a public currency until casts of

them were made and sold in the early 1960s. Johns seems to have met Duchamp at the beginning of 1959, and started collecting works by him in the early 1960s. For more matters of fact about Johns' interest in and relations with Duchamp, see Roberta Bernstein, *Jasper Johns' Paintings and Sculptures 1954–1974*, pp. 60–68. It should be clear from my essay that I doubt that Duchamp's readymades have any place as resources for Johns' light bulb and flashlight sculptures. Nor do I see any connection between Duchamp's work and the painted bronzes of 1960.

45 Note this exchange in Leo Steinberg, 'Jasper Johns: The First Seven Years of His Art', *Other Criteria*, p. 32: 'He was asked why his bronze sculpture of an electric light bulb was broken up into bulb, socket, and cord:

    A :   Because, when the parts came back from the foundry, the bulb wouldn't screw into the socket.
    Q :   Could you have had it done over?
    A :   I could have.
    Q :   Then you liked it in fragments and you chose to leave it that way?
    A :   Of course.'

46 Alan R. Solomon, 'Jasper Johns', *Jasper Johns* (New York, 1964), p. 18; (London, 1964), p. 23.

47 Ibid., (New York, 1964), p. 18; (London, 1964), pp. 23–24.

48 Max Kozloff, *Jasper Johns*, p.32.

49 Roberta Bernstein, *Jasper Johns' Paintings and Sculptures 1954–1974*, p. 53.

50 Max Kozloff, *Jasper Johns*, p. 32.

51 Painting the reflector and the bulb is one way that the difference between the sculpture of the flashlight and the base might be signified. This is particularly effective in the case of *Flashlight III* that was cast in bronze in 1987. Taking *Flashlight III* into bronze removed the material and structural differences between the flashlight and its base and made the near-unity of the piece into a unity. The aluminium paint on the bulb and reflector draws attention to that bit of the object's – the flashlight's – seeming 'literalism' and marks the original difference, albeit by adding a metonym for reflection and light.

52 For more on sculp-metal see *working in sculp-metal* (Pittsburgh, Pennsylvania: Sculp-Metal Company, n.d.).

53 Stuart Preston, 'Real and Surreal in the Week's Exhibition, Dada Revisited', *New York Times*, 25 October 1959, II, p. 23.

54 Richard Shiff, 'Constructing Physicality', *Art Journal*, Spring 1991, p. 46. For more of Shiff's writing on touch see 'Performing an Appearance: On the Surface of Abstract Expressionism' in *Abstract Expressionism: The Critical Developments*, ed. Michael Auping (New York, 1987), pp. 94–123; 'Picasso's Touch: Collage, Papier Collé. "Ace of Clubs" ', *Yale University Art Gallery Bulletin* (1990), pp. 38–47; and 'Cézanne's Physicality: The Politics of Touch' in *The Languages of Art History*, ed. Salim Kalim and Ivan Gaskell (Cambridge, 1991), pp. 129–180.

55 Ibid.

56 Jasper Johns in conversation with the author, 22 September 1995. It was important for Johns that here, on the surface of *Flag*, 'something be a "thing" that could be identified and not just texture… It was an attempt to anchor it in reality… it's in keeping with most of my work that precedes that'. On how textural and textual 'things' were used to make *Flag* (1954–1955), see Fred Orton, *Figuring Jasper Johns*, pp. 110–131.

57 *The New American Painting* was the title of a show of the work of sixteen Abstract Expressionists organised by the International Program of the Museum of Modern Art, New York. During 1958 and 1959 it travelled through eight European countries before returning for presentation at the museum. It is often overlooked that Alfred H. Barr Jr was the first person to write about Abstract Expressionism as the 'triumph' of American painting. See the last paragraph of his 'Introduction' to *The New American Painting*, exh. cat.; The Museum of Modern Art, New York (1959; Arno Reprint, 1972), p. 19: 'To have written a few words of introduction to this exhibition is an honour for an American who has watched with deep excitement and pride the development of the artists here represented, their long struggle – with themselves even more than with the public – and their present triumph.'

58 According to Michael Crichton, *Jasper Johns*, p. 38, 'Johns denies that his earliest paintings were a reaction to Abstract Expressionism. He says that he didn't know enough, hadn't seen enough, to make such a response.' But note also these two, not necessarily contradictory, recollections of Robert Rauschenberg: (1) 'Jasper and I used to start each day by having to move out from Abstract Expressionism.' – quoted by Mary Lynn Kotz in *Rauschenberg: Art and Life* (New York, 1990), p. 90; and (2) 'We were the only people who were not intoxicated with the Abstract Expressionists. We weren't against them at all, but neither one of us was interested in taking that stance. I think both of us felt that there was too much exaggerated emotionalism around their art.' – in Paul Taylor, 'Robert Rauschenberg: "I can't even afford my own works anymore".' *Interview* (December, 1990), p. 90.

59 The 'metaphorics of masculinity' comes into this essay from T. J. Clark's 'Jackson Pollock's Abstraction' in

Reconstructing Modernism: Art in New York, Paris and Montreal 1945–1964, ed. Serge Guilbaut (Chicago and London, 1990), p. 229.

60 For an extensive discussion of the early writing on Johns' way of working with wax and newsprint scrap and how it described a sexuality of texture and touch see Fred Orton, *Figuring Jasper Johns*, pp. 110–131.

61 Johns quoted by Michael Crichton, *Jasper Johns*, p. 43.

62 'Interview with Jasper Johns' in Christian Geelhaar, *Jasper Johns: Working Proofs* (London, 1980), p. 44.

63 Jasper Johns interview with G. R. Swenson, 'What is Pop Art?', Part 2, *Art News* (February 1964), reprinted in *Pop Art Redefined*, ed. John Russell and Suzi Gablik (London, 1969), p. 82. Johns made two versions of *Painted Bronze* (ale cans), the first in 1960, the second in 1964. The first *Painted Bronze* (ale cans) is in the collection of the Museum Ludwig, Cologne, the second is in the collection of Jasper Johns. The sculptures, which are both dated 1960, are so similar that they are referred to here as if they are one and the same.

64 See 'Conversation. Leo Castelli: "Who Knows When Another Epiphany Will Occur" ', *Art News* (April 1991), p. 75, where Castelli explains that though he was very involved with the Abstract Expressionists, when he had a gallery he 'tried to detect that other thing and stumbled on Rauschenberg, Johns and Twombly.'

65 See Peter Fuller, 'Jasper Johns Interviewed', Part I, *Art Monthly* 18(July–August 1978), p. 7:
Peter Fuller. Well, take de Kooning specifically. Why do you admire him so much? What did you learn from him?
Jasper Johns. I think more interesting is what I have not learned from him, which seems to be there. (Laughs.)

66 A. H. Barr Jr, 'Introduction', *The New American Painting*, p. 15.

67 Ibid. For glimpses of the 'scene' at the Cedar Street Tavern see Irving Sandler, *The New York School: The Painters and Sculptors of the Fifties* (London and New York, 1990), pp. 30, 32, and 33.

68 Max Kozloff, *Jasper Johns* , p. 31. Kozloff probably saw the second version of 1964 being painted.

69 Roberta Bernstein, *Jasper Johns' Paintings and Sculptures 1954–1974*, p. 54.

70 John Gruen, *The Party's Over Now: Reminiscences of the Fifties – New York's Artists, Writers, Musicians, and their Friends* (New York, 1972), pp. 190–195 reprinted in *David Smith: Sculpture and Drawings*, ed. Jörn Merket, exh. cat.; Whitechapel Art Gallery (London, 1987), pp. 168–169. See *David Smith: Sculpture and Drawings*, p.168.

71 Ibid.

72 Brad Gooch, *City Poet. The Life and Times of Frank O'Hara* (New York, 1993), p. 448. See the photograph reproduced in *David Smith: Sculpture and Drawings*, p. 14.

73 Quoted in Brad Gooch, *City Poet. The Life and Times of Frank O'Hara*, p. 448.

74 Robert Motherwell in *David Smith: Sculpture and Drawings*, p. 168.

75 Jasper Johns interview with G. R. Swenson, 'What is Pop Art?', Part 2, *Art News* (February 1964), reprinted in *Pop Art Redefined*, ed. John Russell and Suzi Gablik (London,1969), p. 82.

76 'Interview' by David Sylvester in *Jasper Johns Drawings*, p. 9.

77 Jasper Johns, 'Sketch Book Notes', *Art and Literature* (Spring 1965), p. 192, reprinted in *Pop Art Redefined* (London, 1969), p. 84.

78 Johns quoted in Vivien Raynor, 'Jasper Johns. "I have attempted to develop my thinking in such a way that the work I've done is not me." ', *Art News* (March 1973), p. 21.

79 Alan R. Solomon, 'Jasper Johns', *Jasper Johns* (New York, 1964), p. 18; (London, 1964), p. 24.

80 For example, ibid., and Roberta Bernstein, *Jasper Johns' Paintings and Sculptures 1954–1974*, p. 55.

81 Walter Hopps, 'An Interview with Jasper Johns', *Artforum* (March 1965), p. 36.

82 Max Kozloff, *Jasper Johns*, p. 31.

83 Michael Crichton, *Jasper Johns*, p. 19.

84 'Interview with Jasper Johns' in Christian Geelhaar, *Jasper Johns: Working Proofs*, p. 44.

85 For further discussion of *Painted Bronze* (Savarin can with brushes) see Fred Orton, Chp. 3 'Figuring Jasper Johns', *Figuring Jasper Johns*, especially pp. 182–198.

86 Clement Greenberg, 'The New Sculpture' in *Art and Culture. Critical Essays* (Boston, 1961), p. 145.

87 Clement Greenberg's 'The New Sculpture', which is dated 1948 in *Art and Culture*, was first published in *Partisan Review*, June 1949, see *The Collected Essays and Criticism, Volume 2, Arrogant Purpose, 1945–1949*, ed. John O'Brian (Chicago and London, 1986), pp. 313–319.

88 Ibid., p. 315.

89 Ibid.

90 Ibid., pp. 315–316.

91 Clement Greenberg, 'The New Sculpture', *Art and Culture*, pp. 143–144.

92 Ibid., p. 143 and 144.

93 Ibid., p. 140.

94 Ibid., p. 145.

95 Ibid.

96 On *High School Days*, see the sketch book note quoted by John Cage in 'Jasper Johns: Stories and Ideas', *Jasper Johns* (New York, 1964) p. 22; (London, 1964), p. 29: 'Make Shirl Hendryx's shoe in Sculp-metal with a mirror in the toe – to be used for looking up girls' dresses. High School Days. (There is no way to make this before 1955.)'

On *Subway*, see Roberta Bernstein, *Jasper Johns' Paintings and Sculptures 1954–1974*, p. 57, who points out: 'Johns said the source for this relief sculpture was an advertisement he saw while riding in the subway. The ad showed a boy in short pants seated between a man and a woman, presumably his parents; someone had written "his" and "hers" on the boy's knees. The ironic humor of the image would have appealed to Johns, and most likely personal associations are connected to the idea that a child is owned by his parents and to the conflicts resulting from the possessive aspects of the parent-child relationship. *Subway* can also be interpreted more generally to imply that each individual has both a male and a female side (although this idea is presented in Johns' typically understated manner, since the knee caps are labeled as if they were objects like bathroom towels rather than parts of a human figure).'

97 Marcel Duchamp, *The Bride Stripped Bare By Her Bachelors, Even*, a typographic version by Richard Hamilton of Marcel Duchamp's Green Box, translated by George Heard Hamilton (Stuttgart, London, Reykavik: Edition Hansjörg Mayer, 1960), n.p.

98 Jasper Johns quoted in Richard Francis, *Jasper Johns* (New York, 1984), p. 98.

99 Frank O'Hara, 'In Memory of My Feelings' in *The Selected Poems of Frank O'Hara*, ed. Donald Allen (New York: Vintage Books, 1974), p. 110 – this edition was reprinted in the U.K. under the title *Frank O'Hara. Selected Poems* by Carcanet in 1961 and by Penguin Books in 1994.

100 At first, the fountain was painted with aluminium paint, but this was worn away by the action of water and weather.

101 In mind here were some remarks of Paul de Man in 'Literary History and Literary Modernity', *Blindness & Insight. Essays in the Rhetoric of Contemporary Criticism*, Second Edition (London, 1983), pp. 142–165 and 'Shelley Disfigured', *The Rhetoric of Romanticism* (New York, 1984), pp. 93–123.

102 This was one of 'three academic ideas' that Johns referred to in his statement for the catalogue of the 'Sixteen Americans' exhibition at the Museum of Modern Art, New York, in 1959. See Jasper Johns, [Statement] *Sixteen Americans*, exh. cat., ed. Dorothy Miller, New York, The Museum of Modern Art (1959), p. 22.

103 See Fred Orton, Chp. Two 'A Different Kind of Beginning', *Figuring Jasper Johns*, for an extensive discussion of Johns' dream and its possible determination in the social and political issues of the day and its likely relation to a recollection that as a boy his father told him in front of Alexander Doyle's *Statue of Sergeant William Jasper*, Madison Square, Savannah, GA, that Jasper was the person they were named for. Sergeant Jasper (1750–1779) served with the 2nd South Carolina Infantry in the Revolutionary War. He distinguished himself during the British bombardment of Fort Sullivan, Charleston when on 26 June 1776 he recovered the fort's flag after it had been shot down and, under heavy fire, remounted it on the walls. He was mortally wounded in October 1779, while rescuing his regiment's colours during the assault on Savannah. Doyle's statue, also known as *The Jasper Monument*, shows Sergeant Jasper raising the colours, and expiring.

104 Frank O'Hara's 'In Memory of My Feelings' is dated 27 June–1 July 1956; it was first published in *Evergreen Review* (1958) and reprinted in *The New American Poetry: 1945–1960*, ed. Donald Allen (New York, 1960). See *The Selected Poems of Frank O'Hara*, ed. Donald Allen (New York: Vintage Books 1974), pp. 105–110.

105 The basic texts on Frank O'Hara and his poetry are: Marjorie Perloff, *Frank O'Hara: Poet Among Painters* (New York, 1977); Alan Feldman, *Frank O'Hara* (Boston, 1979); and Brad Gooch, *City Poet. The Life and Times of Frank O'Hara* (New York, 1993).

106 Brad Gooch, *City Poet. The Life and Times of Frank O'Hara*, p. 334.

107 See ibid., 'Love', pp. 329–376.

108 Jasper Johns in conversation with the author, 22 September 1995.

109 Brad Gooch, *City Poet. The Life and Times of Frank O'Hara*, p. 332.

110 Frank O'Hara, unpublished letter to Johns, 15 July 1959, cited in Marjorie Perloff, *Frank O'Hara: Poet among Painters*, p. 203 nn. 41 and 44.

111 Frank O'Hara, 'Joe's Jacket' (10 August 1959) in *The Selected Poems of Frank O'Hara*, pp. 151–152.

112 Frank O'Hara, 'What Appears To Be Yours' (13 December 1960) in *The Collected Poems of Frank O'Hara*, ed. Donald Allen, pp. 380–381.

113 Only one collaborative print was accomplished, *Skin with O'Hara Poem*, 1963–1965, lithograph, published by Universal Limited Art Editions, Inc., West Islip, N.Y. The O'Hara poem is 'The Clouds Go Soft', see *The Collected Poems of Frank O'Hara*, p. 475. O'Hara also offered Johns 'Poem (The Cambodian Grass is Crushed)' and 'Bathroom', see *The Collected Poems of Frank O'Hara*, pp. 555–556. James Cuno, 'Voices and Mirrors/Echoes and Allusions: Johns' *Untitled, 1972*' in *Foirades/Fizzles: Echo and Allusion in the Art of Jasper Johns*, p. 232 n. 42, pointed out that the coming together of the poem and the print 'was prompted by Francine du Plessix who edited an anthology of artists' responses to poems for an issue of *Art in America*. Du Plessix had written to twenty-two American painters during the winter of 1964 asking them to make a work in response to a contemporary poem of their choice. Three New York painters chose O'Hara but Johns was the first to reply (not just with the choice of O'Hara but the first to reply to the project at all – a sign of his interest in poetry) and so he got his choice.' See *Art in America* (October–November 1965), p. 24. The character and kind of Johns' response was not only a sign of his interest in poetry.

114 This drawing, *Memory Piece (Frank O'Hara)*, 1961, is illustrated in Nan Rosenthal, Ruth E. Fine and Amy Mizrahi Zorn, *The Drawings of Jasper Johns*, fig. 39a, p. 166.

115 Frank O'Hara, 'Dear Jap' (10 April 1963) in *The Collected Poems of Frank O'Hara*, pp. 70–71 and Roberta Bernstein, *Jasper Johns' Paintings and Sculptures 1954–1974*, pp. 82–83.

116 Brad Gooch, *City Poet. The Life and Times of Frank O'Hara*, p. 185.

117 Frank O'Hara, 'In Memory of My Feelings' in *The Selected Poems of Frank O'Hara*, p. 108.

118 See Roberta Bernstein, *Jasper Johns' Paintings and Sculptures 1954–1974*, p. 226 n. 1: 'In 1970, when Johns was arranging a chronological listing of his works [with Roberta Bernstein], he commented, "the mood changes," when he got to 1961'.

119 Marjorie Perloff, *Frank O'Hara: Poet Among Painters*, p. 141.

120 Ibid.

121 Ibid.

122 Alan Feldman, *Frank O'Hara* (Boston, 1979), p.92.

123 Marjorie Perloff, *Frank O'Hara: Poet Among Painters*, p. 142, and Alan Feldman, *Frank O'Hara*, p. 92.

124 Frank O'Hara, 'In Memory of My Feelings', *The Selected Poems of Frank O'Hara*, p.110.

125 The x-ray photographs of Johns' *In Memory of My Feelings – Frank O'Hara* are illustrated in Fred Orton, *Figuring Jasper Johns*, illustration 22, p. 65.

126 Roberta Bernstein, *Jasper Johns' Paintings and Sculptures 1954–1974*, p. 84.

127 *'In Memory of My Feelings': A Selection of Poems by Frank O'Hara*, ed. Bill Berkson (New York: The Museum of Modern Art, 1967), a commemorative volume of O'Hara's poetry illustrated by thirty American artists.

128 Marjorie Perloff, *Frank O'Hara: Poet Among Painters*, p. 215 n. 23.

129 For more thoughts on Johns' use of cutlery and what it may mean, see James Cuno, 'Jasper Johns', review of *Jasper Johns: A Print Retrospective* by Riva Castleman, *Print Quarterly*, IV, (1987), pp. 91–92 and James Cuno, 'Voices and Mirrors/Echoes and Allusions: Jasper Johns *Untitled, 1972*' in *Foirades/Fizzles: Echo and Allusion in the Art of Jasper Johns*, pp. 220–221.

130 Calvin Tomkins, *Off the Wall: Robert Rauschenberg and the Art World of Our Time* (New York, 1980), pp. 197–198.

131 Marjorie Perloff, *Frank O'Hara: Poet Among Painters*, p. 210 n. 5.

132 Riva Castleman, *Jasper Johns: A Print Retrospective*, exh. cat.; The Museum of Modern Art, New York (1986), p. 24.

133 Susan Sontag, 'In Memory of their Feelings' in *Dancers on a Plane: Cage. Cunningham. Johns*, exh. cat.; Anthony d'Offay Gallery, London (1989), p. 23.

134 Ajit Mookerjee, *Tantra Art: Its Philosophy and Physics* (Kumar Gallery, New Delhi, New York, Paris, 1966; Basle, 1971), see plate 9, p. 30. The painting is also illustrated in *Tantra*, exh. cat. by Philip S. Rawson; Hayward Gallery, London (1971), no. 237, where it is titled *The Terrible Devata Samvara who has seventy-four arms with his female wisdom (sakti) with twelve arms*, Nepal, gouache on cloth, 17th century. It is reproduced in colour in *Dancers on a Plane: Cage. Cunningham. Johns*, p. 8.

135 See the entry for *Dancers on a Plane*, 1980, in *The Tate Gallery 1980–82: Illustrated Catalogue of Acquisitions*, (London, 1984), p. 146 and Richard Francis, *Jasper Johns*, p. 95.

[136] 'Interview with Jasper Johns' in Nan Rosenthal, Ruth E. Fine with Amy Mizrahi Zorn, *The Drawings of Jasper Johns*, p. 82.

[137] See Ajit Mookerjee, *Tantra Art: Its Philosophy and Physics*, p. 30.

[138] Johns quoted in Michael Crichton, *Jasper Johns* (London, 1994), p. 62.

[139] Mark Rosenthal, *Jasper Johns: Work Since 1974* (London, 1989), p. 44.

[140] For more on the *Dancers on a Plane* pictures and their relation to *Cicada* of 1979, *Tantric Detail I* of 1980, and *Tantric Detail II* and *Tantric Detail III* of 1981 see Fred Orton, *Figuring Jasper Johns*, pp. 162–182.

[141] Susan Sontag, 'In Memory of their Feelings' in *Dancers on a Plane: Cage. Cunningham. Johns*, p. 13.

[142] Roberta Bernstein, *Jasper Johns' Paintings and Sculptures 1954–1974*, pp. 116–117.

[143] Johns quoted in Charlotte Willard, 'Eye to I', *Art in America*, 54 (March–April 1966), p. 57.

[144] Jasper Johns, 'Sketchbook Notes', *Juilliard*, 3, winter 1968–1969, pp. 25–27; reprinted in Richard Francis, *Jasper Johns*, pp. 109–111.

[145] Jasper Johns in conversation with the author, 22 September 1995

[146] Ibid.

[147] In 1968, the title page of Ted Berrigan's *The Sonnets* (1967) was silkscreened onto *Screen Piece 3 (The Sonnets)* and one or two pages of a newspaper were screened onto *Screen Piece 4* (Robert and Jane Meyerhoff Collection).

[148] Jasper Johns in conversation with the author, 22 September 1995.

[149] See Charles Baudelaire, *The Salon of 1846*, 'Why Sculpture Is Tiresome' in *Art in Paris 1845–1862. Salons and Other Exhibitions*, trans. and ed. Jonathan Mayne (London, 1965), p. 111: 'Sculpture has several disadvantages which are a necessary consequence of its means and materials. Though as brutal and positive as nature herself, it has at the same time a certain vagueness and ambiguity, because it exhibits too many surfaces at once. It is in vain that the sculptor forces himself to take up a unique point of view, for the spectator who moves around the figure can choose a hundred different points of view, except for the right one, and it often happens that a chance trick of the light, an effect of the lamp, may discover a beauty which is not at all the one the artist had in mind – and this is a humiliating thing for him. A picture, however, is only what it means to be; there is no way of looking at it than on its own terms. Painting has but one point of view; it is exclusive and absolute, and therefore the painter's expression is much more forceful.'

[150] Michael Fried, 'Art and Objecthood', *Artforum* (June 1967); reprinted in *Minimal Art: A Critical Anthology*, ed. Gregory Battcock (New York, 1968), pp. 117–147.

[151] Ibid., p. 145 and 146.

[152] 'Interview with Jasper Johns' in Christian Geelhaar, *Jasper Johns: Working Proofs*, p. 50.

[153] Ibid.

[154] Johns quoted by Michael Crichton, *Jasper Johns*, p. 42.

[155] Ibid., p. 48.

[156] Note the drawing *Sketch for the Critic Smiles*, 1959, illustrated as fig. 30a in Nan Rosenthal, Ruth E. Fine and Amy Mizrahi Zorn, *The Drawings of Jasper Johns*, p. 148.

[157] Max Kozloff, *Jasper Johns*, p. 10.

[158] Jasper Johns in conversation with the author, 22 September 1992. Johns did the plaster casting himself.

[159] Ibid. At the end, Kozloff is quoting from Paul Valery's *Degas, Manet, Morisot*: 'All the arts live by words. Each work of art demands its response; and the urge that drives man to create – like the creations that result from this strange instinct – is inseparable from a form of "literature," whether written or not, whether immediate or premeditated. May not the prime motive of any work be the wish to give rise to discussion, if only between the mind and itself?'

[160] These remarks on 'theory' come out of my reading of Wlad Godzich's 'Foreword. The Tiger on the Paper Mat' and Paul de Man's 'The Resistance to Theory' in *The Resistance to Theory* (Minneapolis: University of Minnesota Press, 1986).

[161] Ibid., pp. 12–13,

[162] Max Kozloff, *Jasper Johns*, p. 9.

[163] Wallace Stevens, 'What We See Is What We Think', *The Auroras of Autumn* in *Wallace Stevens. Collected Poems*, (London and Boston, 1984), p. 460.

[164] William Carlos Williams, 'Book One', *Paterson* (1946–1958), *Selected Poems* (Harmondsworth, 1976), p. 231.

[165] 'Interview with Jasper Johns' in Christian Geelhaar, *Jasper Johns: Working Proofs*, p. 48.